Women & Children of the Cut

by
WENDY FREER
with 42 illustrations

RAILWAY & CANAL HISTORICAL SOCIETY

First published in 1995
by the Railway & Canal Historical Society
Registered office: Fron Fawnog, Hafod Road, Gwernymynydd, Mold, Clwyd CH7 5JS
Registered charity no.256047

ISBN 0 901461 18 0

Designed and typeset by
Malcolm Preskett
Printed in England

COVER ILLUSTRATION
A pair of narrow boats, *Nuneaton* and *Bedworth,* head north
on the Grand Union Canal by Nash Mills in Hertfordshire.
Steered by Mr and Mrs Ken Ward on 13 May 1967,
they are carrying cargoes of wheat
destined for Wellingborough.

Contents

ACKNOWLEDGEMENTS

THIS BOOK was adapted from a thesis presented for the degree of PhD at the University of Nottingham. I would like to thank Professor S.D. Chapman who was my supervisor during my time at Nottingham. Thanks are also due to the staff of numerous libraries and record offices, particularly to the staff of the Public Record Office at Kew. I would also like to thank Dr Ian Donnachie of the Open University who helped and encouraged me to embark on a study of the social history of canals.

My thanks are also due to a number of people who helped with the preparation of the manuscript: Mr Cliff Miller who read and offered advice on an early draft, Mr Oliver Smart and Mr Grahame Boyes of the Railway & Canal Historical Society who co-ordinated the publication process, Mr Richard Dean who drew the diagrams and map, Dr Mike Pegg who edited the manuscript and Mr Malcolm Preskett for the design, typesetting and artwork. I am very grateful to Mr Alan Faulkner who put his photograph collection at my disposal and my thanks are due to the National Waterways Museum and Robert Wilson for permission to use illustrations from their collections.

Lastly, but by no means least, I should like to thank my husband who has supported me throughout my studies.

Preface

THE social and economic circumstances of canal boat life have received little serious attention from historians and the experiences of women and children have been particularly neglected. This book sets out to describe the everyday life of the families who lived wholly or mainly on long-distance narrow boats but it also goes further than this. There is no attempt to 'romanticise' the boat people and their way of life. Instead, every effort has been made to set their experiences and circumstances firmly in context and to make accurate comparisons with other occupational and social groups. Canal-boat work is one of the few occupations employing a significant number of women and children where no specific legislation was ever enacted to control the hours and conditions of their work. Child labour was common far into the twentieth century and children were denied even the most elementary education. One of the main purposes of this book is, therefore, to look at why this was so, what attempts were made to remedy the situation, and why they failed. There are other books about canal life, but few have concentrated on the lives of women and children. One notable exception is Sheila Stewart's splendid book *Ramlin Rose* which draws on her many conversations with boat women as well as on her extensive research among the literature of the canals. It is hoped that *Women and Children of the Cut,* drawing as it does on the little known wealth of source material amongst the files of the government departments of the day, will form a useful companion work.

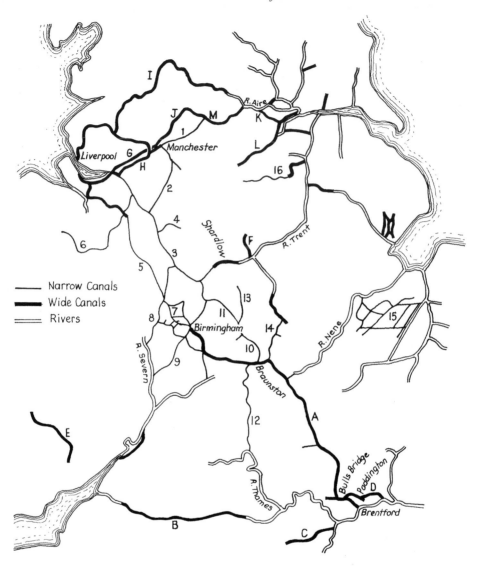

NARROW CANALS

1 Huddersfield Narrow
2 Macclesfield
3 Trent & Mersey
4 Caldon
5 Shropshire Union
6 Llangollen
7 Birmingham canal navigations
8 Staffordshire & Worcestershire
9 Worcester & Birmingham
10 North Oxford
11 Coventry
12 Oxford
13 Ashby
14 Leicester (Grand Union)
15 Middle Level
16 Chesterfield

WIDE CANALS

A Grand Union
B Kennet & Avon
C Basingstoke
D Regents Canal & Paddington
E Monmouthshire & Brecon
F Erewash
G Manchester Ship
H Bridgewater
I Leeds & Liverpool
J Rochdale
K Aire & Calder
L Sheffield & South Yorkshire
M Calder & Hebble

— ONE —
The Canal Carrying Trade

LITTLE serious attention has been paid by historians to the social and economic circumstances of the men, women and children who, for nearly 200 years, operated canal boats on the English inland waterways system. Indeed, it will come as a surprise to some that canal carrying continued to be regarded as a serious and important form of freight transport by certain sectors of British industry until as recently as the Second World War. Even after that, canal carrying managed to survive on a small but commercially viable basis until the late 1960s. Canal carrying still survives on the wide waterways of the north east of England, but on the canals of the Midlands and the South, long-distance carrying by narrow boat came

1 *(left)*. The main waterways of England and Wales at the end of the 19th century

2 *(above)*. Mrs Martha Humphries on *Freda* in April 1940. *Robert May / Alan Faulkner Collection*

to an end by about 1970. Even so, canal enthusiasts and one or two small experimental companies continue carrying in narrow boats to this day.

The organisation of the trade

EVER SINCE the building of the first industrial canals in England in the second half of the eighteenth century, the primary function of inland waterways was the bulk transport of heavy raw materials, particularly coal. In the last decades of the eighteenth century, such heavy goods accounted for well over half of the total traffic. This was still the case over 100 years later. Coal alone accounted for 45% of the traffic carried on the main waterways in 1905.[1] The remainder of the traffic also consisted mainly of bulky low-value materials such as pig iron and sand together with grain and food stuffs. Regional variations existed. In Cheshire, for example, 61% of the traffic carried in 1913 was salt and chemicals[2], and in other regions cargoes reflected the predominant local industries.

Not only did heavy low-value materials comprise the bulk of canal traffic, but most of it travelled over fairly short distances – probably less than 20 miles on average.[3] Much of the tonnage carried by inland boats would have consisted of ships' cargoes being lightered around major ports, especially on the Thames, Mersey, Humber and Severn. Some long-distance traffic would have been carried by canal and river during its journey but, on the whole, there was a fairly clear demarcation line between river and canal traffic in terms of vessels and labour force. For one thing, it was unsafe for narrow-beamed, flat-bottomed canal boats to venture into tidal waters and most river vessels were too big to penetrate far into the canal system. The labour forces too kept themselves distinct. Being of more ancient establishment and because of the greater danger involved in navigating natural waterways, river boatmen tended to regard themselves as superior to canal boatmen. Many river boatmen had passed through a proper apprenticeship system and had their own highly exclusive trade organisations.

In addition to the clear distinction between river boatmen and canal boatmen, many differences existed within the canal carrying trade itself. The canals themselves differed greatly from one another in width, depth and size of lock. This led to such a great variety of boats and operating systems that it is impossible to generalise about canals or canal-boat people. However, for the sake of clarity, some broad classifications can be made. Most canals fall into the category of either a narrow canal or a broad canal. This has less to do with the width of the canal itself, and more to do with the size of the locks and bridge holes. Locks on narrow canals take boats of approximately 7ft in width and up to 72ft in length (although some take only slightly shorter boats). Wide canals have locks which can accommodate either two narrow boats side-by-side, or a wide boat of up to 15ft beam. These restrictions on the size of the boat had enormous implications for the economics of canal carrying; the less cargo space available, the less commercially viable a boat becomes. Furthermore, where the crew had to sleep on board there were obvious implications for living and working conditions. Some idea of the differ-

ence in cabin layout, for example, can be seen in FIGS 13 and 14 in chapter 3.

In the Midlands the canals were mainly of the narrow type. The links with the Mersey, through the industrial districts of the Black Country and the Potteries, were also narrow canals. The route to London was at first by the narrow Oxford Canal and the Thames, but later the Grand Junction Canal made a better link. During the 1920s and 1930s the canals between London, Birmingham and Langley Mill were amalgamated to create the Grand Union Canal which would have carried the wide boats as far as the outskirts of Birmingham. However, reconstruction plans were never completed and broad-beamed boats rarely worked further north than Tring. The wider locks did, however, allow narrow boats to be worked through in pairs.

Travelling from the Midlands to the Humber was once by narrow canal as far as Shardlow and thence by the river Trent which took wide boats. From Birmingham to the Bristol ports one travelled by narrow canal as far as the river Severn at Stourport or Worcester, although links could be made via the river Avon. In the north of England, the majority of canals were wide. This, together with the fact that they linked some of the most important ports and industrial districts of the nineteenth century, made them more prosperous than the narrow canals of the Midlands and the rural canals of the South. On some larger canals, steam tugs were used to tow trains of wide boats. The most successful application of this idea was on the Aire and Calder where special containers known as 'Tom Puddings' were pulled in trains.[4]

The boat families with which this book is concerned were found mainly on long-distance narrow boats plying around the Midlands and between there and the four major estuaries – the Thames, the Mersey, the Severn and the Humber. Some, however, lived on wide boats, both in the North and on the London canals and not all were concerned with long-distance traffic. Some worked for large carrying companies, some for smaller ones, whilst others worked for themselves and were known as 'bye-traders' and later as 'number ones'. Some worked for the canal companies themselves, where these companies had their own carrying department. Even where this was not the case, for

3. Harry Berrisford posing on *Phoenix,* middle lock, Buckby, 1910.
National Waterways Museum

example with the Oxford Canal Company, the company sometimes employed a few boatmen, possibly for maintenance purposes.[5]

During the nineteenth century, another important division within the canal carrying trade was that between the fly-trade and the slow-trade.

The slow-trade carried heavy, low-grade materials such as coal, other minerals, refuse etc. It was made up of a large number of boat owners, most of whom carried in a relatively small way. Many were substantial industrialists, colliery and foundry owners etc., who operated a few boats to meet their own transport needs. It was common for such men to own a few boats themselves and to hire others as and when the need arose. Some boats were owned by the boatmen themselves.

Most slow-boats operated over short distances and the men and boys who operated them returned home to their families most nights. Some of these boats had a makeshift cabin where a boatman could get some shelter from the weather and perhaps cook a simple meal. Long-distance slow-boats had proper cabins and were operated sometimes by a man and boy, sometimes by a family.

There were no fixed hours of work on the canal. Most slow-boats worked 12 to 14 hours a day for as long as work was available, although some owners made their boatmen tie up on Sundays.[6] Where the boat was owned by the boatman himself there were no restrictions on the hours he and his family could work and, although it was usual for slow-boats to tie up for some part of the night, it was not unknown for 'bye-traders' to work non-stop once loaded.

Slow-boats did not operate to a strict timetable and would usually wait until they had a full load before setting off. In the nineteenth century, and in many cases far into the twentieth, the boat would be pulled by a single horse which would not be changed during the journey. Often the horse had to be provided by the boatman himself. A man could set himself up in this trade with little initial capital other than that required to buy a boat and horse and it was well suited to the small operator who would pick up a cargo where he could and make the most cost-effective use of his boat.

Larger carriers often used these owner-boatmen, or 'bye-traders', as Frederick Morton explained in 1920.

If a man takes a load from Stourbridge district to London, a load of firebricks … we very frequently load that man's boat back for him; he will carry the cargo for us and we pay him a haulage charge for carrying it on our account … and we pay the tolls.[7]

The fly-trade was the express service of the carrying trade. It carried general merchandise, manufactured goods, perishables and higher-value heavy cargo in relatively faster vessels. Fly-boats operated between the main manufacturing districts and the ports, especially between Birmingham and London and Birmingham and Liverpool. They were also found on the larger canals of northern England. Fly-boats were lightly loaded with not more than 10 or 14 tons, compared with 30 or 35 tons for a fully-loaded horse-drawn narrow boat in the slow trade. They also departed regularly according to a fixed timetable, whether fully loaded or not. They were crewed by a team of four men who worked day and night in shifts. To speed their passage, the horse was changed every 35 miles or less and they were given priority over other boats whilst underway.[8] Because of the long distances and more valuable cargoes involved, extensive warehousing premises were required in various parts of the country together with offices, stabling and private wharves. In order to maintain regularity and speed of service a large number of boats and an even larger number of horses would have to be bought and maintained and, with light-loading, sometimes run at a loss. A large workforce of agents and clerks was needed to deal with the daily running of the business. The administration of long-distance canal-boat carrying was notoriously complicated. Each canal was privately owned. Each had its own

particular system of tolls and special discounts and each had to be dealt with separately. Carriers complained that:

… so long a time is spent in correspondence [with the canal companies] that the traffic has passed before a rate has been arranged for it.[9]

Considerable financial resources were required to operate the complex systems of credit allowance which carriers offered to customers in order to combat competition from other forms of transport and only companies of substantial means were allowed credit on tolls by the canal companies. This was a concession which some small companies found it particularly hard to do without. Nor were speed and regularity the only considerations, as Joseph Baxendale, a partner in Pickfords explained:

… if Persons have Property of consequence they would wish to put it into the hands of Men of Property, so that if there is any loss they can get, if not the whole, at least 10 shillings in the Pound, but if they are put into the Hands of a Man not worth a Bawbee, they can get nothing, so that they always in the Case of valuable Goods, do send them by Men of Property.[10]

Thus it was very difficult for anyone of modest means to engage in the fly-trade or at least to stay in it for very long. For this reason, fly-carrying tended to be concentrated in the hands of the big public carriers such as Pickfords who operated large fleets of boats and employed hundreds of men and horses. At its height in 1838, Pickfords' fleet consisted of 116 boats and 398 horses.[11]

After 1840, much of the fly-trade traffic had been lost to the railways and most of the big carriers either closed down or, as in the case of Pickfords, transferred their business onto the railways. Several canal companies started large carrying departments at this time following an Act of Parliament in 1845 which merely legalised that which several had already been doing for some time, namely, carrying on their own waterways. Their motive was to save what they could of the merchandise trade as more and more private carriers left the canals.

The Grand Junction Canal Company formed a carrying department in 1847 and picked up what was left of Pickfords' trade together with some of their boats and premises. By 1853, the Grand Junction Canal Company was carrying 75% of all the traffic on its own canal.[12] The venture was not a

4. Boat family aboard *Benjamin* around the turn of the century.
Alan Faulkner Collection

success and had to cease trading in 1876. The breach was filled by a new company, the London & Staffordshire Carrying Co., a forerunner of Fellows Morton & Clayton, which was to become the premier long-distance carrier of the canals between the late-nineteenth century and 1948.

The Shropshire Union Railway & Canal Company started carrying in 1845 and by 1883 the company's boats and those of the larger traders were carrying 70% to 80% of the traffic on their canal.[13]

During the last quarter of the nineteenth century, the fly-trade lost more and more traffic to the railways. By the last decade of the century, fly-boats still operated on the larger northern canals, such as the Aire & Calder, and the Shropshire Union Railway & Canal Carrying Company were still running a number of fly-boats from Staffordshire to Liverpool to meet ships. However, Fellows Morton & Clayton ran only a few and these at a loss.[14]

In the twentieth century, the distinction between the fly-trade and the slow-trade became less important. Up until the Second World War boats sometimes worked fly. Horses continued to be used for some short-distance work, especially in the West Midlands, but after the First World War, diesel-powered motor-boats began to be used for all grades of traffic. These boats often towed an unpowered boat known as a 'butty boat'.

Despite declining fortunes, many people found that it was still possible to make a living out of the canal carrying trade and for more than a century after the end of their so-called 'golden-age', that is the first four decades of the nineteenth century, canals continued to fulfil a useful, if diminishing role in the transport system of the country.[15] This was achieved despite fierce competition from rivals employing superior technology, lack of public investment and the enormous shortcomings of the canal system itself with its inconsistency of gauge and lack of co-operation between one canal company and another and between canal companies and carriers.

Families begin to work on canal boats

IT SEEMS to be still widely believed that families did not begin to work on canal boats until the middle of the nineteenth century. The reason was thought to be the onset of competition from the railways which so impoverished the canal boatmen that they could no longer afford to maintain their families ashore or hire a crew to help them with their work. It was supposed that, as a result, they gave up their cottages on the canal-side and took their families on board as a source of cheap labour.

Not only modern historians have made the mistake of thinking this, but even some contemporary observers of the late-nineteenth century believed it to be the case. Charles Bowling, a factory inspector, said in 1875:

Thirty years ago no women or children lived in canal boats and that most probably their doing so has been the result of the competition of the railways , which has compelled canal companies to convey their traffic at a cheaper rate.[16]

Evidence that this was not the case was first put forward by Harry Hanson in 1975.[17] He pointed to a book by John Hassell in which the latter described a journey he made on the Grand

5. Boats *Fornax* and *Ra* being gauged at Norton Junction.
National Waterways Museum

Junction Canal in 1819. Hassell described boats entering Blisworth tunnel where:

… the men throwing off their upper garments and lighting up their lantern, gave the helm for steerage to the women, one or two females generally attending each boat.[18]

In 1832, a member of the Select Committee on the Observance of the Sabbath referred to boatmen, remarking 'they are in the habit of having women on board with them continually are they not?'[19] By 1841, when a House of Lords Select Committee was investigating Sunday working on canals and railways, it was obvious from the comments of several witnesses that some boatmen had long been accustomed to having their families with them on the boats.[20]

Unfortunately, it is very difficult to estimate how many women and children were to be found on canal boats during the nineteenth century. The census enumerators did not take full personal details of people sleeping on inland boats until 1861, although they were counted in the totals for earlier census years. However, the figures for women and children are particularly unreliable and difficult to interpret. Women sleeping on board with their husbands were not usually included in the occupational tables and the same applies to children below the age of ten or twelve. Women and children were included in tables for people sleeping on board inland boats but these do not, of course, include people working on day boats. The census of England and Wales shows that the number of people working on all inland boats and barges reached its peak in 1851. Of the 32,617 men employed,[21] however, nearly half were lightermen and flatmen working on rivers, estuaries and in docks and were not canal boatmen at all. TABLE I is an attempt to eliminate the majority of river boatmen by taking figures from the census summary tables only for those counties through which the main canals run.[22] Judging by the number of females sleeping on board inland boats on the night of the census, women probably made up no more than 15% of the canal-boat work force in 1851. This appears to have risen to about 20% by 1871. A survey conducted by the Canal Association in 1884[23] found that the number of children sleeping on canal boats in May of that year was approximately 5,700. Over 2,000 of these

were infants, but most of those who were old enough to make any contribution to the running of the boat, would have been working.

By 1931, the census tables show that the number of men employed on all inland boats had fallen to 21,113 but probably fewer than half were canal boatmen. Women probably formed no more than 15% of the canal-boat labour force at that time and it is likely that the ratio had fallen to below 10% by the 1950s.

From 1870 onwards, the number of children living and working on canal boats caused much controversy. Figures given by social reformers such as George Smith of Coalville were highly suspect, whilst those published by the Board of Education were collected in such a haphazard manner as to render them almost useless. Based on the various estimates available, it is possible that as many as 2,500 children were to be found living on canal boats during the inter-war years. This had probably fallen to a few hundred by the time the Second World War was over.

Women were not found on all canal boats. They worked mainly on long-distance boats in the slow-trade. Fly-boats did not employ women or girls but young boys were to be found employed as hands on all sorts of canal boats.

The question of why women and children began to work on canal boats is not difficult to answer. In the pre-industrial economy, in agriculture and cottage industries, the family had commonly worked together as a single economic unit based on the labour of all its members. Even when industrialisation gave rise to larger-scale manufacturing, family units did not at once disappear from the workplace as families had been able to work together in some early factories. Thus, given that most women and many children who went to work on the canals did so to assist male relatives, there was much about this that was traditional and natural.

The way in which boatmen were paid encouraged families to take to the boats. In most cases, only the captain or steerer was employed by the carrying company or boat owner. He was given a sum of money sufficient to enable him to hire his own crew and cover certain other running expenses. Increasing the family income, whilst keeping down the running costs of the boat, was

TABLE I.
Estimated numbers of males and females working on canal boats 1851–1951*

(Source: Census of England and Wales, 1851–1951, population tables and occupational tables for selected counties
(see note 22)

* There appear to be no figures available for woman sleeping on board inland boats and barges in 1911.

■ Men ▥ Women

bound to be a factor in deciding whether to take the family on board.

Later in the nineteenth century, factory and workshop legislation restricting the employment of women and children in many trades drove some into areas of employment not yet controlled in that way. Mainly this meant the sweated trades but it is not unreasonable to suppose that some took to the canals.

Judging by the number of females sleeping on board on the night of the censuses, the use of family labour was to some extent a regional custom. Family labour was far more common on the Grand Junction Canal, the Oxford Canal and in the Black Country, less common on the wide canals of Lancashire and Yorkshire and on the route between Birmingham and the Severn. It seems that some boatmen preferred to have their families on the boat rather than suffer long separations. Indeed, in the last decades of the nineteenth century and the early part of the twentieth, when attempts were made to pass legislation banning women and children from living on canal boats, boat people made it known that they were fiercely opposed to any measure which threatened to break up their family life.

Even where economic motives were uppermost in the minds of boatmen who hired their own families as crew, it was not necessarily the case that

they could no longer afford to maintain them ashore. Most boatmen, including those who took their families with them on board, were said to have houses on the bank.[24] These houses might be used by the family from time to time and locked up when they went away – the 1881 census enumerators' books for the village of Braunston in Northamptonshire contains references to several such houses.

Other sources give a clue about another motive for having families on board. The Select Committee on Sunday Trading in 1841 heard that women went with their husbands on the boats to 'keep an eye on them' and stop them indulging in heavy drinking or taking on board prostitutes who were said to hang about at tunnel entrances among other places. This concern with the influence of women on the morality of the boatmen can be found in later government enquiries, such as the Select Committee on the Canal Boats (1877) Act Amendment Bill in 1884. In 1920, a government inter-departmental enquiry into the practice of living-in on canal boats was set up. The committee was very concerned with the moral influence of having women on board the boats and most witnesses agreed that where married women accompanied their husbands on board it was a good thing on grounds of morality and the additional home comforts which could be afforded to the men.

— TWO —

Working Life

B Y FAR the most striking and significant feature of canal-boat work was its irregularity. Whether because of alternating periods of slack and brisk trade, the influence of weather and the seasons, or because of the way in which the work was organised, irregularity was as characteristic of canal-boat work in the nineteenth and twentieth centuries as it was of work in general in pre-industrial England.

The most serious disruptions were due to ice in winter when the trade might be completely halted for several days and, occasionally, several weeks. Because of the difficulties of maintaining water supplies to a man-made, still waterway, severe drought could force boats to be light-loaded or might close a section of the canal completely. Floods could also cause delays.

By far the most important cause of irregular

6 *(above). Falcon* and *Stone* at the New Warwick Wharf, Birmingham in October 1939 with Alice Kendall at the tiller of her father's butty boat.
Birmingham Evening Mail

work patterns was the way in which the work was organised. Usually, a boat crew would be given orders to load and deliver a particular consignment and then left largely unsupervised to carry out the task. Once loaded, the length and intensity of the working day was, in theory at any rate, entirely up to the captain. Methods of payment were complex but in general terms, the captain was paid a fixed rate for every ton delivered with an allowance known as trip money which took into account any difficulties of the particular journey. There was, therefore, a financial incentive to deliver goods as quickly as possible which resulted in long working days and, in the case of a long journey, a long working week once the boat was under way.

Once the consignment was unloaded at its destination, the boat crew would hope to receive new orders straight away but all too often this did not happen. There might be a delay of a day or more before the boat could be unloaded. The boat and its crew might have to lie idle for a day or more before another load could be found or it might have to travel empty for several days in order to pick up a fresh cargo from elsewhere. Delays might also occur at bottle-necks such as tunnels and locks and more time could be lost waiting for repairs. Even a hard-working boatman might spend no more than 55% of the year actually working. If he was not paid for running his boat empty, as was usually the case until the inter-war period, an even smaller percentage of his time was spent engaged in remunerative employment. Although the boatman worked less time than the worker in manufacturing industry, his official rest-days were far fewer. Moreover, whilst after the First World War the average worker laboured for eight or nine hours per day, with working days spread evenly throughout the twelve months, the boatman's time was divided into periods of intense labour of perhaps twelve to fifteen hours per day, alternated with periods of enforced idleness.

Fly-boat crews worked day and night in shifts. In theory, two men should have been resting while two worked the boat which should have afforded the crew a reasonable period of rest. In practice, it was often necessary for the whole crew to be at work to get the boat underway or speed it through a flight of locks. Witnesses at the Royal Commission on Labour in 1892 testified that fly-boatmen regularly worked 100 hours per week and that up to 70 hours might be worked without any proper rest.[25] Sixteen- and eighteen-hour shifts were common and periods of rest were said never to exceed two hours.[26] Here is how one man described a typical period of work:

I commenced to work at seven o'clock on the Wednesday Morning. That was the time turned out. We were at the graving dock. We worked there till half past five at night. Then we had to go down to the warehouse and we commenced to load at a quarter to seven. We finished loading at a little after half past eleven. It was half twelve before we got down the two locks and at one o'clock the ebb of that tide came and we went down to Liverpool and discharged cargo the next day ... It was nine when we got alongside. I had to go to the office then to look after the boats to discharge the cargo. At three o'clock we were discharged at Alexander Dock. We had to come back from there to Cornstone and we commenced to load again at a quarter to seven at night and we finished at half past two in the morning and at about a quarter to three we were going back again to Runcorn. We had to navigate to Runcorn and it was seven o' clock on Friday night

when we finished work. That was from Wednesday morning ... I had not any sleep.

Slow-boat crews did not work throughout the night, but they often started work between three and five o'clock in the morning and carried on until eight or nine o'clock at night. In 1841, slow-boatmen were said to work fourteen or fifteen hours out of twenty four.[27]

State regulations on the employment of women and children gradually shortened the hours of employment and improved the working conditions of workers in many other industries. Beginning with textiles, by 1878 legislative control had been extended to mines, metal-working, printing, paper-making trades and small workshops but no legislation ever attempted to regulate the hours and working conditions in the canal carrying trade.

In addition to long shifts, it seems to have been common throughout the nineteenth century for boatmen to work seven days a week at times, although periods of enforced idleness were also inevitable. John Crowley, a fly-boat operator, saw no necessity for a rest-day at all. He thought that the overnight stoppage of the boat should provide boatmen with sufficient rest from their labours.[28] Even in the twentieth century there was no fixed rest-day for narrow-boat men. They usually carried on until a particular trip was finished and would continue work for as long as work was available. This could mean several weeks without an official day off, although the frequent delays on the canal meant that the work was not entirely relentless.

Not until 1919 did the reduction of hours in other industries begin to affect the canal carrying trade. In that year the Canal Control Committee, a Board of Trade body which had governed the canals since they came under government control in 1917, ratified an agreement which laid down a 48-hour week for most canal employees. It was felt, however, that the nature of the work would make this impossible for narrow boatmen who were granted a 33⅓% increase in wages in lieu.[29]

Sometimes, conditions in outside industries had a more direct effect on the working hours in the carrying trade. Following a dispute in May 1920, some Midlands boatmen carrying coal, brick, stone, lime, slag, ashes and pig-iron between collieries, works and power stations, secured an agreement

7. A stoppage at Cowroast on the Grand Junction Canal *c.*1915.
National Waterways Museum

which stipulated a 54-hour week (nine hours per day) with some payment for overtime.[30] However, it seems unlikely that this agreement would have resulted in a real reduction of hours if the depression of trade and disputes in the coal industry had not substantially reduced traffic. An industrial court heard the following year that the average number of hours worked by those boatmen in October 1920 was 55.2 per week, yet the men were employed on average only for about three quarters of their time.[31] On the Leeds & Liverpool Canal in Lancashire, the introduction of a five-day week in the coal industry meant that only two boat trips per week were possible instead of five per fortnight.[32]

On the Shropshire Union Canal, which was owned by the London & North Western Railway Company, pressure from the National Union of Railwaymen to bring canal workers into line with railmen led to a 48-hour week being introduced on an experimental basis for flatmen and boatmen in July 1920.[33] Boatmen were said to dislike this arrangement as it had the effect of reducing their

wages, but before the issue could be finally settled the company decided to close its carrying department.

By 1945 there were still no set hours for long-distance narrow boatmen. By this time even the unions seem to have recognised the impossibility of trying to implement a fixed working week without a radical reorganisation of the industry.[34] A boatman interviewed in August 1959 claimed that he still often worked eighteen hours a day.[35] This is possibly an exaggeration but other boatmen interviewed around the same time confirmed that a twelve-hour day was normal and a longer one not uncommon.[36] However, one has to take into account that such hours were not worked every day.

Manually-operated locks, primitive cargo handling techniques and poor management meant that the work was arduous, slow and inefficient. Some wharves had mechanical aids such as cranes or chutes but much of the work had to be done with shovel and wheelbarrow. As trade declined and the canals became more dilapidated, wharf facilities often deteriorated too, making cargo handling more laborious. David Blagrove, who worked a pair of narrow boats in the early 1960s complained of:

… the ludicrous comparison of an articulated lorry with timber packed in lengths being unloaded in minutes with fork lift truck while we puffed and grunted in the traditional manner.[37]

Blagrove also complained about the time-consuming and wasteful loading of grain at Brentford where:

… boats had to hang about at the depot until lighters were available. Then the operation was both labour-intensive and slow and finally a fair amount of grain was wasted or spoiled. Had a couple of hundred-ton silos been built, the grain could have been sucked into them, stored and released into boats as required and all with the minimum of time and grain wasted. However, such plans were repeatedly frustrated by lack of capital and obstruction from unions who claimed that the men would lose jobs.[38]

Tim Wilkinson[39] also turned his hand to canal boating for a short while after the Second World War. Both he and Blagrove complained of the frustrations of loading and discharging at large ports where the restrictive practices of dock workers caused more hindrance than help. Both came across works depots where it was the rule that railway wagons and lorries had preference over canal boats when it came to loading and unloading. Looking at the work with the eyes of outsiders, they both felt that cargo handling was one of the most frustrating and inefficient aspects of the job and one where much improvement could have been made.

Name of vessel *ALFRED* Belonging to *WORCESTER*				Description *CANAL BOAT*	
NAME	CONDITION	AGE MALE	FEM	OCCUPATION	PLACE OF BIRTH
George Collis	married	21		captain	Worcester
Mary Ann Collis	married		21	wife	Worcester
Clara Collis			3		Worcester
George Hemming	unmarried	11		assistant	Worcester

Name of vessel *FANNIE* Belonging to *WORCESTER*				Description *CANAL BOAT*	
NAME	CONDITION	AGE MALE	FEM	OCCUPATION	PLACE OF BIRTH
Benjamin Davis	married	61		captain	Stroud, Glouc.
Mary Davis	married		58	wife	Pike, Worcs
Benjamin Weaman	unmarried	15		mate	Birmingham

Name of vessel *PROSPER* Belonging to *GLOUCESTER*				Description *CANAL BOAT*	
NAME	CONDITION	AGE MALE	FEM	OCCUPATION	PLACE OF BIRTH
Giles Smith	married	42		captain	Gloucester
Ann Smith	married		34	wife	Standish, Glouc.
John Bernard	unmarried	15		mate	Elmore, Glouc.

TABLE 2. Extracts from the Census of England and Wales, Birmingham. 1861
(Source: Census of England and Wales 1861 PRO RG9/2139)

8. A young child apparently operating lock gates.
Robert Wilson Publications

The role of women and children in the workforce

WHERE the boat was also the family home, it is often very difficult to say whether the women and children found on board were actually operational members of the crew or not. Even on all-male boats only the captain was employed by the carrying company. The hiring of a crew, whether they were hired hands or the boatman's family, was a matter for the captain.

One of the reasons for the presence of women on board was to attend to cooking, laundry and cleaning and where the women were also the mothers of young children it was natural for them to have their offspring with them on the boats. Hanson[40] felt that even where women were required from time to time to steer the boat, they were often still not proper members of the crew. He used census data similar to that in TABLE 2 to argue that women on narrow boats were sometimes supernumerary. His argument rested on the idea that a boat would be operated by two people, either a man and a mate or a man and his wife so that where a couple employed a mate, this rendered the labour of the woman superfluous. However, the census data in TABLE 3 seems to refute this. It shows that on some boats, mates were employed even when the son of the family was in his teens. A youth of seventeen or eighteen would certainly not have been supernumerary and so it seems that extra hands were hired even when there were already two able-bodied adults on board. Given the nature of canal-boat work, the cramped conditions on board and the way boats operated, it seems likely that any able-bodied person above the age of about eight, and sometimes younger than this, would be expected to make a significant contribution to the operation of the boat.

So what sort of work did women and children do on the boats? Tom Cubbon, commenting in 1928, gave the impression that boat women could turn their hands to anything when he said of them:

… when anything went wrong, or anyone was in a fix, there they were, with steadfast eyes looking under dark brows ready to lend a hand, throw a rope, or lever you off a shallow with a spare tiller.[41]

Women certainly helped with steering the boat and driving the horse. They also operated the locks and, where necessary, hauled the boats by hand in and out of them. In the *NSPCC Annual Report* for 1925/6, one boat woman commented 'we boat women often get injured through raising lock paddles and working lock gates'. The *Co-operative News* for 15 January 1910 contained a reference to a lone woman with a boy of about fifteen and a girl of about twelve, hauling a pair of boats filled with china clay through the locks at Runcorn. In some places, where sailing boats were used, some 'bow hauling' was necessary. The boatman Harry Fletcher[42] recalls his childhood on a sailing keel before the First World War when:

Mother often had to steer the boat if Dad was busy with other jobs and when there was no wind and no money to hire a horse, she had to help to haul the keel by hand.

Women were not usually in charge of the boat although there were some women captains. The *Journal of the Birmingham Canal Company* for 1777/8 and Government boat registers for 1795 contain references to a Hannah Hipkiss who captained various boats during this period.[43] However, census enumerators' books contain few references to boats in the charge of women. Where women are found in charge, they are rarely described as 'captain', which in itself says something about the status of women, if only in the eyes of the Victorian enumerators.

Where women were in charge of boats, this was usually because the captain had died and his widow had decided to step into the breach. One boat-woman claimed in 1877 that four out of every six boats coming from Wigan were captained by widows.[44] This claim is not supported by census records but it does seem to be true that women did not usually rise to the position of captain except where the death of their husbands either compelled them or gave them the opportunity to do so.

Children too made their contribution to the full range of jobs on board. Of course, one should not be surprised to find large numbers of young children working long hours in harsh conditions before the twentieth century. In the past, children were often compelled to leave home between the ages of seven and fourteen to begin work as domestic servants, labourers and apprentices in the homes of other families. Despite the growth of protective legislation, until the end of the nineteenth century, most working-class children had short childhoods, some ending as early as the age of four if their parents worked at home. Not only did children begin to work at an early age, but many were treated with indifference and neglect. What makes canal-boat children different from most is that in their case, illegal child labour and educational deprivation continued until well into the second half of the twentieth century.

Of course, the presence of a child on a boat does not necessarily mean that it was in employment there. The majority of children found on canal boats were living there with their parents. Whether, or to what extent, they were required to help operate the boat in such circumstances is not easy to say.

Where children are found on boats other than those of their parents it is safer to assume that they were operational members of the crew but the census enumerators' returns indicate that in the second half of the nineteenth century children did not leave the family boat to work for outsiders until the age of ten years, and more usually between the age of twelve and fourteen. Many boys worked with

Name of vessel *EDWARD and KING ARTHUR* (2 boats) Description *CANAL BOAT, BRICK TRADE*				Size *30 TONS EACH* Belonging to *PADDINGTON*	
NAME	CONDITION	AGE MALE	FEM	OCCUPATION	PLACE OF BIRTH
John Reid	married	47		master	St Albans
Elizabeth Reid	married		46	wife	Chesham
Caroline Reid	unmarried		18		Berkhampstead
Joseph Reid	unmarried	17			Berkhampstead
Peter Owen		15		mate	Brinkley, Staffs

Name of vessel *NOT NAMED* Belonging to *PADDINGTON*				Description *GENERAL TRADE*	
NAME	CONDITION	AGE MALE	FEM	OCCUPATION	PLACE OF BIRTH
Gabriel Evans	married	50		master	Coventry
Hannah Evans	married		48	wife	Coventry
John Evans	unmarried	19		mate	Birmingham Richard
Brown		32		mate	Birmingham

TABLE 3. Extracts from the Census of England and Wales, Paddington. 1861
(Source: Census of England and Wales, 1861 PRO RG9/3 pp.189–258, RG10, pp.143–50)

9. A young boy leading a horse-drawn boat on the Oxford Canal between Browsover Mill and Vicarage Hill, Clifton, *c*.1895. The Great Central Railway bridge is seen being constructed. It was demolished in 1975.
Rugby Public Library / Railway & Canal Historical Society Collection

their fathers, either on his boat or another boat in tandem with his. Some boys between the ages of ten and fourteen can be found working as mates on fly-boats. On Worcester Wharf, Birmingham, in 1871, two boats were employing as crew members fourteen-year-old girls, not apparently members of the captains' families.[45] Most unusual of all, the census enumerators' returns for Paddington Canal in 1861 show one Richard Livers, aged twelve, together with his brother, John, aged ten, in charge of two 30-ton boats. The master of the vessel is given as Richard Livers, who may have been the father, but there was no sign of his presence on any other boat in the district that night so it would appear that the children were working the boat themselves. In a nearby boat was one Emma Livers, aged eleven years, described as 'in charge of canal boat' the only other occupant being her three-year-old brother William.[46]

These are, however, exceptions. The bulk of the child labour force was made up of children living and working on their parents' boats and thus, the number of child crew members remains highly elusive. The only body to have attempted to quantify them is the NSPCC and their efforts did not get underway until the beginning of the twentieth century.

This organisation published a report on canal-boat children in 1910 in which it was reported that a special inspector had seen boys as young as six years of age and girls of eight driving the horse and steering the boat. Gate paddles were thought by many to be too heavy to be worked by young children but this inspector reported seeing boys of seven and girls of twelve operating locks.

Several witnesses who gave evidence to a government enquiry into living-in[47] on canal boats in 1920/1 agreed with the NSPCC. Most informed sources agreed that children helped to some extent with the operation of the boat but there was controversy about whether what they did actually constituted 'employment', 'manual labour', or 'child labour'. The Reverend Ward of the Incorporated Seamen and Boatmen's Friend Society and Mr R.A. Knight of the London Mission both agreed that children helped by driving the horse but told the Committee that they considered this to be no more than the sort of assistance any child might be expected to give about the house.

Everyone agreed that the operation of lock-gate paddles constituted manual labour but many thought it a physical impossibility for a child to perform such a task. John Griffiths, canal carrier, stated in his written evidence to the Committee that women and children provided between a half and two thirds of all the labour in the long-distance carrying trade but when questioned by the Committee he said that a child would not be able to open gate paddles before the age of twelve or fourteen years. William Hackett, the NSPCC Inspector for Canal-Boat Children, claimed, however, that he had seen a child of seven 'draw the paddles by jerks, one cog at a time'.

Not all boat families lived permanently on board the boat and child labour was not confined to those that did. A register for boat boys attending Archdeacon Street Council School, Gloucester in 1919[48] shows that even in an area where family labour on boats was less prevalent, boys from boat families, seemingly without exception, were taken away from school to work on the boats from about eight or nine years of age. According to the teacher, most of these Gloucester boat families had houses in the town where the mother, daughters and younger children continued to live while father and sons went away with the boats.

Not everybody was in favour of women working on canal boats, even within the industry. Trade unionists in many industries had been against the employment of women from the 1840s onwards. The men clearly wanted women to stay out of the competition for jobs and they were also concerned that employing women would lower

wages. They rarely admitted this, however, and usually made excuses about the unsuitability of women for canal-boat work. William Speed who represented the Upper Mersey Watermen and Porters' Association told the Royal Commission on Labour in 1892 that he wished the employment of women on boats to be prohibited.[49] He denied that this was in order to create better employment prospects for men, claiming that his objection was on the grounds of humanity in that it was not the sort of work in which women ought to be engaged. He said:

We have in some instances women who have charge of craft … actually captains of them, and we find when we are brought in contact with these in the dark at night that it is very dangerous to life in some cases. A short time ago, outside in the river Mersey, with a woman on board of a craft, one of our own men had to get overboard from his craft to save her life and to save the craft itself.

Elllis Gatley[50] of the same union also objected to women and girls being employed on boats on the grounds that the work was unwomanly. One of the Commissioners pressed him to explain why this was but he would only say that women were not good at steering. They caused accidents and it was not good for them to work day and night. He did not think it was necessary to consult the women themselves but then neither did he think it necessary to consult the men who had their wives on board.

By the 1940s attitudes seemed to have changed little. During the Second World War, a few, largely middle-class women trainees, were recruited to undertake war service by operating canal boats. The scheme started in 1941 when Daphne March and a woman friend began operating a boat on the Severn. When the government, who were once again controlling the canals under war-time arrangements, suggested training crews for other regions, the idea met resistance from within the industry. In the West Midlands it was reported:

The short-distance carriers view the heavy character of their work as ruling out the employment of British

10. Mrs Clara Wilson on board *Snipe* loading timber at Brentford. *Bill Wilson / Alan Faulkner Collection*

women, whilst the long distance carriers have, in some cases, made limited experiments with women, but not much progress has so far been made … The representatives of carriers present expressed themselves averse to the employment of women on grounds of general unsuitability.[51]

Despite this, labour shortages forced some carriers to consider employing women. A training scheme was started on the Grand Union Canal but it remained a very limited affair. In 1943 it was reported that fifty pairs of boats were lying idle on the canals through lack of crews yet the Grand Union Canal Carrying Company was aiming to train women crews for only fifteen. Even this turned out to be over-optimistic. By February 1945 it was reported to the Central Canal Committee that there were sufficient women trained or in training for only nine pairs of boats.[52]

According to one of the trainers, one of the chief difficulties with women crews on the Grand Union was that they could not earn enough money, at least not at the outset. This was partly because the crews were larger than normal and partly because even with these crews they could not earn as much as experienced boat people. Boats also had to be modified to accommodate these women who were not used to the privations of canal-boat life. Mrs Butson set out the problems and alterations they had in mind in a letter to the Director of Canals, Sir Osborne Mance in 1942:

We would be content with a lavatory and a basin (if space could be found) in the engine room and a very tiny cabin in the bow … A tank for water would also be a blessing … The double bed is a very inconvenient arrangement and there is not enough room to use the seat as a second bunk unless more leg room was provided by cutting away the stern partition of the cabin … We would also like to pick our own boat as we know of one not in use which is free of bugs.[53]

Canal-boat work was more popular with women in the North West. It was reported in February 1945 that fifty-seven applications for training with the Leeds & Liverpool Canal Company had been received. This exceeded the training facilities available, however, and as the recruitment publicity also attracted nearly a hundred applications from men, few of these aspiring boat women ever actually found themselves at the tiller.[54]

Income

THE methods of remunerating boat captains were so various and elaborate that it is difficult to get an accurate idea of the average level of money wages at any time throughout the period in question. Most boat captains were not paid a fixed weekly wage but according to the length and difficulty of the journey and the value and tonnage of the cargo. Almost invariably, no two trips ever attracted the same payment. Furthermore, the diversity of canals and boats makes it difficult to generalise about the income of the labour force as a whole.

Before the twentieth century there is no evidence that full sets of agreed trip and tonnage rates were ever written down; if they were, none seems to have survived. It is possible to find copies of such agreements dating from the early years of the present century. However, even where they exist, canal-boat work was so extremely irregular, with stoppages of days or even weeks occurring owing to vagaries of the weather or delays in loading and unloading, that it is difficult to work out the average weekly wage from such documents.

An additional difficulty is that no fixed payment was made to the captain and each member of the crew. Only the captain was employed by the company, and he was left to hire his or her own crew and fix his own terms and rate of pay with them. Account also has to be taken of certain running costs which had to be met out of the payment made to the captain. These might include the cost of finding and keeping a horse or horses and the cost of ropes.

To get any idea at all of the level of money wages among boat crews one has to rely on estimates given by contemporaries – boat owners, canal inspectors and even boat people themselves.

For example, in 1841 Richard Heath,[55] a carrier from Stourport, stated that he paid his fly-boat captains on average £9 per week. Out of this the captain had to find three horses and a crew of three as well as paying for various running costs. He could expect to net, on average, 30 shillings a week. Figures given by Philip Bouverie of the Grand Junction Canal Company and Joseph Baxendale of Pickfords' Canal Carrying Company confirm

11. Mrs Clara Wilson on board *Bunting* in the summer of 1960 waiting to unload at Great Bridge, Tipton.
Max Sinclair / Alan Faulkner Collection

Heath's statement.[56] Slow-boat captains were paid less. A figure between 15 shillings and 30 shillings per week, excluding the cost of the horse, was suggested in 1841 by Josiah Hayes, an agent of the Staffordshire & Worcestershire Canal. It probably resulted in an average of 20 shillings a week net.[57] This represented a money wage considerably above that of agricultural labourers of the time, and in fact boatmen's money wages were about on a par with coal miners and cotton spinners, two of the best-paid sectors of the nineteenth-century working class.

For most boat people, money and real wages rose in the first seven or eight decades of the nineteenth century. Evidence given by factory inspectors in 1875 shows that slow-boat captains were earning between 25 shillings and 42 shillings per week after expenses.[58] This figure excluded the cost of the horse but not the cost of hired labour where that of the family was not used. Fly-boat captains were receiving about £4 17s 6d gross, or about 37s 6d net. This compares very favourably with the pay of other manual workers. After this time, the fly trade did less well, but in the slow trade, up to 1885, the rate at which real wages rose was above the national average.

After about 1890, boat people, like other working people, experienced a down-turn in money wages. Nevertheless, their income continued to compare well with other workers in the old staple industries. In 1906 a Board of Trade enquiry[59] into earnings found that canal boatmen on piece rates earned on average 32 shillings per week net. Engineering workers at that time were earning 28 shil-

25

lings, coal miners 32 shillings and agricultural labourers 18 shillings per week.

During the First World War most industrial workers enjoyed significant increases in money wages. At first, canal labour was left far behind and there was much discontent in the industry.[60] After 1917, however, when inland waterways came under government control, wages rose in what one member of the Canal Association described as 'the most reckless fashion'.[61] By 1920 they stood, according to one government source, at 100% above pre-war levels.[62] However, retail prices were rising so fast at this time that they cancelled out any increases in money wages.

After the war an initial boom was quickly followed by wage cuts in the early 1920s. In 1921 an industrial court ruling removed the wage increases granted to Midland boatmen in 1920[63] and a 5% decrease was imposed on Fellows, Morton & Clayton boatmen in 1923.[64] However, retail prices were falling so sharply at this time that real wage levels were maintained and even increased between 1921 and 1923. Money wages for boat people reached a peak around 1930 and in the following decade they fell by something like 30%. Nevertheless, money wages continued to compare favourably with those of some other industrial workers. For example, in 1936 narrow-boat captains on the upper Trent were receiving on average 55 shillings a week,[65] coal miners 45 shillings and agricultural workers 35 shillings weekly. However, boat people worked a considerably longer week than the average industrial worker.

In addition to these apparently high rates of money wages, those who lived permanently on board had no rent, rates, fuel or travelling expenses to find. Poaching from canal-side fields, fishing from the canal itself and 'perks' from the cargo which might be used by the boat crew or exchanged at locks for other goods also enhanced the crew's income.

There is little evidence about whether women were paid differently to men. Where a woman was a member of the crew, in most cases the captain was her husband or father and the question of how much she was paid does not really arise because crew members belonging to the captain's family were not paid a separate wage. Where wage agreements have survived, there is no suggestion that women captains were paid less than men. Hannah Hipkiss certainly seemed to do well out of boating. Hanson worked out that in 1777/8 she earned at least £2 per week net throughout the year, a figure well in excess of many men's earnings at the time. However, a report written by the Medical Officer of Health for Paddington in 1926 to the Chief Canal Boat Inspector states that 'the earnings of boatmen vary between £2 and £3 per week and in the case of women working alone about 30 shillings'.[66]

Paying boat captains by tonnage or trip rates had its advantages and disadvantages for boat people. It raised the status of the captain above that of a wage-earner and indeed, a boat captain was given a great deal more responsibility than a factory hand. Not only was he expected to work largely without supervision, but he was responsible for the cargo whilst in transit and held accountable for any damage or loss. Richard Heath of Stourport, testified to the fact that only men of good character and a little education were employed as captains, men who could be trusted not to pilfer the cargo, could read way-bills and give proper receipts for goods delivered.

Among the draw-backs was the fact that it allowed employers to avoid taking full responsibility for members of their work force and allowed leading employees to exploit their assistants, be they hired hands or members of their own family. The system whereby only the captain was officially employed by the company meant that in the twentieth century the captain was the only member of the crew entitled to any cover or benefit under the workmen's compensation and National Insurance laws. In 1924 Fellows, Morton & Clayton agreed to be responsible for the employment of the crew which gave them entitlement to the benefits of these Acts. This was extended to the crews of the Grand Union Canal Carrying Company in 1937. Despite this, only on the route between Birmingham and the Severn did it ever become the custom for the carrying company to pay crew members a separate wage. Such a system was fiercely resisted in other districts despite pressure from the trade unions and the government. Along with the dilapidated condition of the canals themselves, it appears to have been one of the main obstacles to the reform of working conditions.

— THREE —
Family Life

FOR THOSE who lived aboard narrow-canal boats, living space was extremely cramped and the ordinary facilities of everyday domestic life were primitive or non-existent. All the aspects of ordinary family life took place in what seem to us today incredibly difficult circumstances. A health visitor commented in 1946:

Sleeping accommodation is limited and they shut themselves in at night. It is mostly overheated from the stove and not one of them had a fire guard. For washing they seemed to use canal water, just carrying sufficient fresh water for drinking and cooking purposes.[67]

However, during the nineteenth century, squalid and cramped living conditions were endured by many ordinary working people. Even during our own century, at least up to the Second World War, such conditions were not exclusive to boat people.

12 *(above)*. A family scene at Birmingham.
Alan Faulkner Collection

The floating home

IN the nineteenth century, a family working a single narrow boat would have had a cabin at the rear of the vessel measuring about 8ft long, 6ft 6in. wide and 5ft high. In addition, many boats had a very small cabin at the front of the boat, little more than a cupboard, where one adult or two children might sleep. Some families worked two boats between them which gave them additional cabin space but even with two boats a family would have had little more than 100 square feet of floor space.

The dimensions and lay-out of narrow-boat cabins do not seem to have changed significantly throughout the two centuries in which they were in use. A good idea of the lay-out can be gained from the plan in FIG.13 and the following passage which appeared in *The Birmingham Daily Mail* on 5 March 1875:

Close to the hatchway is the usual fat little stove in full

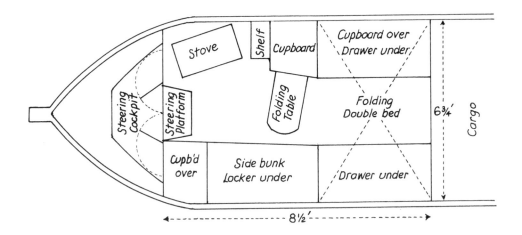

13 *(above)*. Layout of a narrow-boat rear cabin

14 *(below)*. Layout of a wide-boat cabin (Sheffield type)

Both diagrams are based on drawings in a memorandum submitted by the
General Council of the Sanitary Inspector's Association to the Ministry of Housing
and Local Government, 1953, PRO ref. HLG/1412

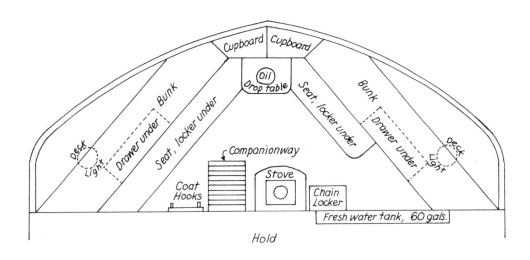

15. The cabin of *Hardy* showing the cooking stove and lace-edged plates used for decoration.
E. W. Paget Tomlinson / Alan Faulkner Collection

glow; opposite this is a 'bunk' or locker – which serves as a wardrobe and sofa – on which three men might sit; at the end of the cabin is another bunk, about three feet wide, the sleeping place, on which the family bed – now boxed up in a cupboard at the end of the bunk – is laid. By the side of the stove is the cupboard that serves as larder, and the door of which forms the dining table. It is fastened up with a wooden button, and when let down it makes a board about a foot and a half long by one foot wide, on which all meals are eaten. Small cupboards, pigeon-holes and shelves are contrived everywhere, and the kitchen and cooking utensils hang gracefully on hooks behind the stove. Every inch of space is utilised.[68]

A similar pattern was followed on all narrow boats although the boats on the route between Birmingham and the Severn seem to have been slightly larger with a better fore-cabin.[69] Wide boats on the lower end of the Grand Junction Canal and in the north of England had larger cabins with a quite different layout (see for example FIG.14).

Overcrowding was often a serious problem. Narrow boats were known to house a man, his wife and several children, as many as ten if some sources are to be believed. The census enumerators' books show that it was not uncommon for boats to contain a man, wife and five or six children. However, this is not very different from the conditions in the overcrowded tenements of many nineteenth-century urban areas. John Liddle,[70] the medical officer for Whitechapel, reported in 1842 that nearly the whole of the labouring population in his district lived in single rooms. In 1887[71] there were London tenements where as many as eight people could be found sleeping in a room measuring 6ft by 8ft. Conditions in rural areas were often no better with examples being given of eleven adults sleeping in a room measuring ten foot square.[72]

Facilities in the cabins for the basic requirements of every day life were minimal. Water was kept in a three-gallon can on the cabin roof and the accompanying dipper bears witness to the fact that much of it was drawn from the canal itself. Canal boats had no sanitary facilities on board and there were few available for their use ashore. Boat people were obliged to use the hedge or the tow-path as a latrine. However, during the first half of the nineteenth century, many working-class people had to share privies and middens which were often in a filthy condition and there are plenty of descriptions of courts and cellars becoming contaminated with human excrement. Although piped water to working-class dwellings had been known from the mid-nineteenth century, it was sometimes so inefficient that it was only on for ten minutes a day.

By 1885 many poor people still had to keep water in tubs in their houses.[73]

Cooking facilities on board were fairly limited with cooking restricted to boiling and a tendency for soot to blow back down the chimney onto the food. Even this was an improvement on the provision in most rural cottages where cast-iron ranges were rarely fitted before the middle of the nineteenth century. Both boat and urban shore dwellers suffered from the disadvantage of dirt and overheating that such forms of cooking caused. Many outside observers commented on the unbearably high temperatures in the boat cabins which rapidly reached the other extreme in the middle of a winter night.[74]

Ventilation of the boat cabin was achieved through the sliding hatch of the door. This was naturally kept closed when the boat was tied up in cold and wet weather, rendering the cabins practically air tight. Again, many working-class houses suffered from poor ventilation in the nineteenth

16. Washing hung out to dry on board boats during a stoppage at Apsley Mill, 1958.
Alan Faulkner Collection

century especially in rural areas where windows were not made to open and holes were sometimes blocked with rags. There was no natural light in boat cabins other than that which came through the open door or hatch. At night sufficient light was emitted by the blazing stove to illuminate the cabin but paraffin lamps were used in addition. This was also the usual means of lighting in other working-class houses until the 1890s when gas lighting began to take its place.

Towards the end of the nineteenth century, living conditions on board canal boats were brought under the regulation of the Canal Boats Act of 1877 and a subsequent Act of 1884 which strengthened and amended its powers.[75] The 1877 Act set up Registration Authorities under which all canal boats used as dwellings were to be registered and issued with certificates specifying the number and sex of persons allowed to sleep on board. It also made provision for local sanitary authorities to inspect boats for infectious diseases and gave School Attendance Committees jurisdiction in educational matters. The Local Government Board drew up regulations in 1878 which stated that boat cabins had to contain 60 cubic feet of free air space for each person above the age of twelve years and not less than 40 cubic feet for each child of twelve years or less. Conditions were laid down concerning the ventilation of the cabin, the provision of cupboards, lockers, a chimney and a vessel for drinking water. The boat was to be kept in a clean and habitable condition and in a good state of repair.

Despite these Acts, overcrowding and poor sanitary facilities continued to be a problem. Inspectors visited boats in order to ensure that no more than the permitted number of people were living on board and to see that the standards of accommodation laid down in the regulations were maintained. However, inspectors only visited the canal five or six times a month so it was easy for boats to be missed. Furthermore, they were not allowed to board boats after 9pm or before 6am which made it difficult to discover the real number of people sleeping on board. Even during the day, overcrowded boats were easily forewarned of the inspector's impending arrival. 'Extra' children could be passed off as visitors or off-loaded onto the bank until the inspector had gone. In some districts boats were hardly ever inspected and there were reports

17. Primitive laundering facilities on the tow-path. *Robert Wilson Collection*

that some unscrupulous owners moved their boats to less well inspected districts if they didn't come up to the standards of the regulations.

During the twentieth century, living conditions on canal boats improved little. The regulations laid down under the Canal Boats Acts were never updated and, with the decline in trade, most carrying companies had little incentive to make improvements. The Grand Union Canal Carrying Company, formed in the early 1930s, seems to have been the only company to make a real effort in this direction.[76] Its new boats, built between 1934 and 1937, were the first to be designed by a naval architect. They were better ventilated and fitted with electric lights run from batteries supplied by the company. This allowed boatmen to acquire a wireless set. However, there was no possibility of enlarging the living accommodation more than a few inches. The overall size of the boat was limited by the size of the locks and all available space on board was needed for cargo if the boats were to be economically viable.

Other improvements during the inter-war period included the replacement of the old type of cooking stove with a new one which incorporated an oven and hot plate.[77] Washing facilities could have been improved by the canal companies but almost nothing was done until it was nearly too late. A stand-pipe for supplying drinking-water was installed by the Grand Junction Canal Company at Brentford in 1889.[78] Other canal-side water taps existed by 1920 and probably before, but toilet facilities remained inadequate. Hackett, the NSPCC inspector and Childs, the Birmingham Medical Officer of Health, both testified in 1920 to the filthy state of urban tow-paths which were used as latrines. Childs claimed that there were some proper WCs for boatmen in Birmingham but Hackett said that they got into such a filthy state that the boatmen would not use them.[79] The Grand Union Canal Carrying Company experimented with the use of chemical closets on its new motor boats, but by 1944, a Ministry of Health official found that 90% of them had been discarded as the crews did not like them.[80]

Washing and laundry facilities on shore were also minimal. In 1926 the canal-boat school at Paddington provided a sink for children to wash in but the education authorities refused permission to provide a bath for fear that children would catch cold.[81] The Boatman's Institute at Brentford provided a washroom for a while and at the Grand Union Canal Company's main depot at Bulls Bridge, the laundering facilities in 1944 consisted of some benches with a roof over, cold water and a coal-fired boiler.[82] These facilities were later modernised but little was done elsewhere. A building at Hawkesbury Junction containing baths and a launderette, opened by British Waterways in July 1960, was said to be the first of its kind in the Midlands.[83]

Primitive as these facilities seem today, they were probably not much worse than those of many urban working-class people on the eve of the Second World War. A survey at that time found that only 26% of households with an income under £300 per annum had piped hot water in 1942. 45% of such households still heated water for bathing and washing of clothes in a copper or in pans on a fire or stove. 27% of these families did not wash their clothes at home and in the poorer districts of London about 80% of families relied on the bag wash, a service which washed clothes but returned them damp and unironed.[84]

Shopping

SHOPPING could be a problem for families who were constantly on the move. They relied on shops near the canal but they were not always well received. In times of shortage, shopkeepers tended to reserve their goods for their regular local customers and, even in times of plenty, boat people sometimes had difficulty obtaining supplies. Mrs Tim Wilkinson[85] said that boat women did not go into any shops, other than a few on the canal-side where they were well-known, for fear of being insulted or thrown out.

There were shops which catered specially for boat people. In the nineteenth century these were often combined with canal-side taverns. In Braunston there was 'a low-roofed tavern, grocer's and butcher's, all in one'[86] and around the Midlands 'dirty, grimy little huckster's shops, half general store and half beer-house [were] pretty frequent'.[87] There were also tailors and boot-makers who catered specially for boatmen. During the First World War, special shops were opened at Skipton and Newark and canteens for boat people were established at Leeds, Stourport, Stewponey and Gravelly Hill.[88]

Church and Chapel

BETTER provision was made for the spiritual needs of the boat people. Public concern for the immoral state of the boating population came to a head in 1839 when a female passenger on a fly-boat was raped and murdered, apparently by the crew. Partly as a result of this, a House of Lords Select Committee was set up in 1841 to see whether canals and railways should continue to be allowed to work on Sundays. The hope was that if Sunday working was banned, boat people would be persuaded to go to church and, as a result, would become much more moral and upright citizens. None of the witnesses knew much about the religious habits of the boating population. One supposed that some went to a dissenting chapel but in most cases, Sunday seemed to be the busiest day of the week in the carrying trade. Witnesses were worried that boat people would not, in any case be able to attend the ordinary parish churches. In many there would not be enough room and there was concern that boat

18. Women aboard the cement boat *Tackley* on 8 February 1911.
Alan Faulkner Collection

people would not have suitable clothes and would have to be separated from the rest of the congregation. One witness believed that the only way to introduce Christian values to boat people was to build special canal-side missions. In fact, by 1841 the Old Quay Carrying Company had already helped to establish Sunday Schools for the men at Manchester and Runcorn and a 'boat chapel' had been established at Oxford, paid for by subscriptions from local inhabitants.[89]

In 1846, a boatman's mission was established in a rented room on the wharf at Worcester Bar (Gas Street Basin), Birmingham by the Incorporated Seamen and Boatmen's Friend Society.[90] From 1879 this Society began to expand its canal-side missions until by 1910 it had thirteen mission centres and twenty-one additional visiting centres. At Brentford, in 1896,[91] the London City Mission established a similar centre and this organisation

also had a Boatmen's Institute at Paddington basin. Both societies held regular religious services for boat people and local townspeople. The missionaries also visited the boats in order to distribute tracts and to exhort the boaters to give up the evils of intoxicating liquor and embrace the faith.

Missions also provided other services. Day schools and Sunday schools were provided for the children and, in the Midlands, coffee rooms offered an alternative to the public house. Tea and coffee were served, books, newspapers and games provided and free washing and letter-writing facilities offered.[92] (A letter-writing service at the local pub cost 3d in 1910.) In Leeds, the mission provided an institute, a canteen, a laundry and a billiard room and at Brentford there was at one time a maternity ward as well as a school and washrooms. At Paddington basin in 1930, the London City Mission, with the co-operation of the canal company, converted an old warehouse into a sort of club. It contained a chapel, a school, a workshop, a men's club, a kinema *(sic)* and a laundry.[93]

In the spirit of the age, canal companies seem to have been more inclined to contribute towards the building of churches and chapels than towards the physical well-being of their labour force. Frank Pick remarked scathingly in his report in 1944 that the Weaver Navigation had 'at a moment of religious enthusiasm … provided churches at its docks, and paid the cost of a vicar or curate, but had failed to supply even lavatories for other human needs'.[94] In 1877 the Shropshire Union Canal Company were persuaded to donate a timber float to be used as a boatmen's mission at Chester and made occasional contributions to its upkeep.[95] This was eventually replaced by a building on the bank for which the canal company provided the site at a nominal annual rent of two shillings and sixpence.[96] The Aire & Calder Canal Company provided the land and building for the mission in Leeds.[97]

Medical treatment

W HEN there was sickness or injury within the family, the itinerant way of life could make it difficult to get medical treatment. Even where boat people overcame their natural reluctance to confront the unfamiliar, often it was not possible to complete treatment or obtain follow-up care when boats spent so little time in one place. Some sort of special provision would have been helpful but, although at least one canal company in the nineteenth century appointed a surgeon and apothecary to attend labourers working on the line of the canal,[98] there is no evidence that such facilities were available to boatmen.

Once again, voluntary bodies tried to meet the need. The Medical Mission, a religious organisation which aimed to relieve the sick poor, set up a clinic in Birmingham near one of the canal wharves.[99] It operated daily between 9am and 5pm in conjunction with the Birmingham General Hospital. It is not known when this mission was first set up but it was still operating in 1944 with subscriptions of threepence or fourpence a week being paid through the Hospital Contributory Association. Non-

subscribers could obtain treatment for a small fee. Fellows Morton & Clayton paid £160 per annum to the Mission and in return for this the Mission agreed to send nurses to the boats to attend confinements.

The London City Mission at Brentford ran a sick-benefit club for a while. In 1925 it had one hundred members and paid out a total of £35 0s 8d in sick benefits.

Under the National Insurance Act 1911, employees were entitled to free medical treatment from a family practitioner although hospital treatment was not included. Dependants of an insured person were not entitled to anything. Boat crews, whether they were the captain's family or hired hands, were not covered by this Act because they were not employed by the carrying company but by the captain himself. Even captains sometimes had difficulty getting the treatment to which they were entitled if they lacked a fixed place of abode.

After the special canal-boat schools at Brentford and Paddington were taken over by the Local Education Authorities in the 1920s, the Public Health Amendment Act of 1907 meant that those children who managed to attend at least received medical examinations. Attempts were made to examine these children once a term and a nurse attended the schools either weekly or daily in order to treat minor ailments and injuries. Efforts were made to reach the parents by visiting the boats and encouraging parents to attend medical examinations at the school where the children's health could be discussed. The nurse at Paddington tried to overcome the boaters' natural reluctance to seek treatment ashore by accompanying parents and children to local clinics. Although improvements in standards of personal hygiene were noticed and some progress was made in persuading parents to obtain dental treatment and spectacles for their children, boat people were still slow to consent to medical treatment and where follow-up visits were necessary, this remained a problem. Of the 42 boat children who visited the dentist in Brentford in 1930, only 25 completed their treatment. One boy was found impossible to treat, although quite why the report does not say.[100]

There were a few people who took a special interest in the health of the boat people. Sister Mary Ward ran a free dispensary for boat people in her own home at Stoke Bruerne until she retired in

1962. In 1944 she was being paid an honorarium of
£2 per week by the Grand Union Canal Carrying
Company, but nothing by the other carrying
companies whose crews used her services. She
performed all the services of a trained nurse and also
some which should have been performed by a
doctor. She worked in the most difficult circumstances with no gas or electricity, no telephone and
she had to pay for her own instruments, drugs,
bandages, disinfectants and the carriage of drinking
water as the village was dependent on well water.[101]
In 1951 she was awarded the British Empire Medal
for her services to the boating community. A retired
doctor living in Stoke Bruerne also took an interest
in boat people and at Bulls Bridge they were
attended by a Dr Smith.[102]

Pregnancy, childbirth and child-care

PREGNANCY and childbirth were particularly
difficult for women who lived wholly on board
the boats as, until the Second World War, delivery
usually had to take place in the cabin. At Brentford,
the London City Mission set up a maternity ward at
the beginning of the twentieth century but it does
not seem to have been used very much. Three
babies were born there in 1902 which was said to be
a record for one year and a few years later the ward
was closed.[103] In 1920 a government enquiry[104]
found that 50% of canal-boat children were born
on board the boat. Nurse Jones, who gave evidence
to the enquiry, recalled some of the times she had
been sent for to attend births in the boat cabins:

They are really in labour when you are sent for, and the
baby is very often born before you get there. They work
up till the last hour getting the boat into the dock.

When asked whether this contributed to the number of stillbirths she said that she thought it did but
added: 'The poor always work very hard to the last
hour ashore and on the boats'.

She described how difficult it was for midwives
to work in the cabins because they could not get a
supply of clean water. The cabins were so cramped
that they could not stand upright and if a doctor
had to attend there was not enough room for
everyone in the cabin. In one case chloroform had

19. Rose Nixon fetching water, March 1956.
Leicester Evening Mail / Alan Faulkner Collection

to be given to the mother and the medical staff were quite overcome with the fumes because of the confined space and lack of ventilation. Nurse Jones said that the mothers were supposed to stay in bed for ten days after the birth but the boats were often gone after two or three.

Ten years later things had changed little. A Ministry of Health doctor reported that the majority of women living on boats had their confinements on board and the birth was attended by a neighbour or a district nurse.[105] The women got up on the third or fourth day after delivery but were said not to engage in any work on the boat for four weeks. In the 1940s the Ministry of Health began to take a particular interest in maternity care and an investigation was begun into the provision for canal-boat women.[106] Arrangements were made for midwives and health visitors to attend the boats more regularly and mothers were encouraged to attend clinics and take advantage of the special provision of free dried milk, fruit juices and vitamins etc. Progress was slow but in 1944 an official reported that:

20. A mug of tea being passed between *Wagtail* and *Crane*. *Jim Payler / Alan Faulkner Collection*

Mothers take hip and other fruit juices willingly but nothing can persuade them to take cod liver oil. They never take vitamins and regard them as 'new-fangled'.

The health visitor at Uxbridge reported in 1946 that most mothers were having their babies in hospital but confinements on board continued and few mothers or infants attended the clinics.

The problems did not end once the baby had been safely delivered. Because the mother was usually busy working the boat, there was no-one to keep a constant eye on the child. As soon as it was able to sit up it would be strapped to a seat, usually on a cushion opposite the cooking stove. Older toddlers were put into a harness and attached to the chimney on the cabin roof. Children in the cabin were in great danger of being injured when the boat was moving. Sudden jolts and bangs at lock entrances could send scalding water from the stove over the children or the children themselves could be thrown against the stove. Outside the cabin there was the obvious danger of drowning and those that were old enough to help with the work stood a good chance of being kicked, stood on or dragged by the horse or injured by the windlass when working the lock paddle gear. Even at night there was danger. Many small infants slept in the same bed as their parents where they were in danger of being squashed and suffocated.

Dr Lilian Wilson visited boats in Brentford on behalf of the Ministry of Health in 1930.[107] She reported that the main causes of infant mortality were convulsions, pneumonia, burns, drowning and overlaying (being squashed by the parents). She visited women on eleven different boats. Most of them had lost children. Several claimed that fewer than half the children they had born were still alive. Mrs Shed on board the boat *Ada* had given birth to ten children, only three of whom were still alive. She said that one had died from knocking over a kettle, one from drowning and one from convulsions but she claimed that she could not remember how the others had died! Two other mothers made similar claims. On the boat *Braunstone* the boatman's daughter had given birth to an illegitimate child which was 'marismic' and seemed unlikely to live. The grandparents would not allow the mother to attend the Infant Welfare Clinic because they 'felt the slur of the illegitimate child'.

21. A family aboard the wide boat *Perseverence*.
National Waterways Museum

Family health

IN 1884, John Brydone, the first Chief Canal Boat Inspector remarked on the hardiness of the boat people,[108] many of whom, he claimed had not known a day's sickness in their lives although, as a Medical Officer of Health pointed out at a later date, 'anybody who had not good health would be compelled to leave the trade'.[109] In fact, the boat population seem to have been remarkably free from the great killer diseases of the nineteenth and early twentieth centuries. One might suppose that children who rarely attended school or came into contact with other children might be less liable than ordinary children to contract the usual childhood diseases. That part of the adult population which lived mainly on board also seems to have been isolated from the general population to an extent which kept them relatively free from serious infectious diseases. Not that boat people enjoyed perfect health. A canal inspector for Goole remarked in 1882 that although only two cases of infectious

disease in canal boats had come to his notice, cases of 'ordinary sickness' had not been rare.[110]

Many of those who commented on the health of the boat people remarked that they were well fed.[111] Their diet was said to consist of beef, bacon, cheese, bread and butter. They drank sugary tea, but always with tinned milk. Later observers commented on the lack of fresh vegetables in their diet. A Ministry of Health official reported in 1944:

I noticed that potatoes were being very thickly peeled and saw no green vegetables in preparation though the value of these appeared to be known. Salads are seldom used and raw vegetables never included in them.[112]

And in 1946 a health visitor reported:

Most of them said that they had fresh vegetables each day but no vegetables were seen cooking, although it was often near the dinner hour when the visit was paid. One family of children were having a meal of bread and cheese, black pudding and drinking tea.[113]

During the Second World War, food rationing was particularly hard on boat families. One Ministry of

Health official reported after an extensive visit to several basins in 1944:

We formed the impression that they were not of the complaining sort but they did tell us that the rationing came rather hard to them. In peace time the boat people are in the habit of having fairly generous supplies of meat and under the present scheme they find it difficult to obtain even the rations to which they are entitled as the regular customers of local butchers get preference when there is any suggestion of shortage of supplies. They also feel the shortage of tea and sugar as they are great tea-drinkers and I found one woman making tea in the afternoon from leaves that had been used at breakfast time. Milk is practically never obtained nor is it obtainable as these birds of passage cannot be registered as regular customers.

The crews do have issued to them emergency travellers cards which they can use anywhere and I am told that this usually works out fairly well except with regard to meat. I heard of one case in Brentford when meat was in rather short supply where a man of about sixteen stone told the missionary at Brentford that in two months the only meat he had been able to get was two breasts of mutton. He tried through the local food officer to obtain more without result but when he sought the advice of the local police he was able to get the ration of meat he was entitled to through the good offices of a constable who accompanied him to the local butcher's shop.[114]

The Grand Union Canal Carrying Company set up a scheme to supplement their crews' food rations.[115] Food parcels containing meat pie, tea and sugar were made available for purchase at their Southall depot and at lock-keepers' premises situated one-day's journey apart along the canal. The company kept a map in their office and represented the movement of boats along it with flags so that they would know how many food parcels to send out. Efforts to persuade other carrying companies to adopt a similar scheme were a failure.

Personal hygiene was yet another problem for families where washing facilities were so primitive and head lice, impetigo and sores were common. Not surprisingly, this was particularly bad amongst people living on refuse boats in Paddington. No doubt the inhabitants of the poorer tenements crowded around the basin were similarly afflicted but conditions on the boats did appear to be significantly worse. When the canal-boat school at Paddington came under the supervision of the nearby St Michael's Elementary School, the headmistress, who would have been accustomed to dealing with children from poor home backgrounds, described the condition of the boat children as deplorable and made special arrangements for the school nurse to make a daily visit to the class.[116] By 1927, standards seem to have been raised to the level of the rest of the school population as Dr Wilson was able to report that sufficient improvement in cleanliness had occurred for the children to join the regular pupils for swimming lessons.[117]

In some places conditions were, on the face of it, more unhealthy than others. The refuse boats operating out of Paddington basin are an obvious example where families slept and ate on boats which were often loaded with foul cargoes. Boat people were not unique in having to live in such conditions, however. Even in the late-nineteenth century it was not unusual for working class people to carry on 'noxious trades' within their living accommodation. Particularly notable occupations were rag picking, matchbox making (in which the paste gave off offensive smells) and rabbit pulling. Costermongers were said to store their unsold and often rotting produce under the bed. Nevertheless, by the late 1920s, the Chief Canal Boat Inspector felt that such conditions should no longer be tolerated and he tried unsuccessfully to have families removed from refuse boats.[118] Surprisingly, the enquiries set in train by his campaign were unable to find any evidence that the children living on these boats suffered any ill health as a result.

* * * * * * * *

CANAL boat work made few concessions to normal family life and one has to wonder at the fact that most boat women managed to care for their families as well as they did. Mothers complained that they had little time for cleaning because of having to help with the boat when on the move. It was only when they were tied up that they were able to clean, cook and feed the family and for many there was always the coal dust to contend with. Children had little time or space to play and, if some contemporary sources are to be believed, they were lucky to survive at all!

— FOUR —
School

SCHOOLING was a very great difficulty for those children who lived permanently or semi-permanently on the boats, but those whose families lived in houses ashore were not unaffected. Attending different schools here and there, wherever the boat happened to tie up, was obviously fraught with social difficulties as well as being of little educational value. The number of children affected is elusive. The Canal Association survey of 1884 found about 2,000 between the ages of five and thirteen years of age sleeping on boats. The Association spokesman believed that a total of about 3,000 school-aged children would be living on boats at that time.[119] During the twentieth century, the number went down as the carrying trade declined.

Between 1,000 and 1,500 were believed to be living on board in the 1920s[120] but this had dropped to no more than 200 or 300 by the 1950s.

In the first half of the nineteenth century there was very little in the way of special schools or classes for boat children although evidently some boatmen were not completely unlettered. Richard Heath,[121] the Stourport carrier, said that many of his captains could read a little owing to the fact that many boatmen sent their children to school in their early years. He was, however, referring to fly-boat captains whose families would have lived in cottages ashore and so had the same chance of going to school as other working-class children. For those travelling with the boat, there were a few Sunday schools established especially for boat people at Runcorn and Manchester.[122] At Oxford, a special day school had been established by 1841, paid for by subscriptions from local inhabitants,[123] and in

22. Julie Ward on board *Ara* at Hillmorton Top Lock. *Michael Black / Alan Faulkner Collection*

Birmingham, the Boatman's Mission on Worcester Wharf offered some schooling from about 1846.[124]

This provision seems poor but, in the first half of the nineteenth century, if canal-boat children attended school irregularly or not at all, they were no different in this respect to many working-class children. A survey carried out in 1818[125] shows that only between 30% and 40% of children in the Midlands were attending school. Many of those who were enrolled did not attend very regularly and in urban and agricultural districts alike, children were taken away from school as soon as they were old enough to be usefully employed. The 1851 Census Report on education estimated that the average length of a working-class child's education was four years. Even if a child did attend school, in many cases, the teaching was of a very low standard. An inspector of 500 textile mills reported in 1838 that he could not name a dozen factory schools where the education offered was systematically good.[126]

Canal-boat children and the education acts

BY 1870, extensions to the factory and workshop Acts had brought some compulsory schooling to children employed in most manufacturing industries and in 1875 this was extended to children employed in agriculture, but children who lived and worked on canal boats still lay outside the provisions of any legislation regulating employment and education. Even the Elementary Education Act of 1870, which authorised the creation of local school boards and gave them the power to make bye-laws compelling school attendance in their districts, could not be applied to children whose place of residence could not be established. The Canal Boats Act of 1877[127] attempted to bring canal-boat children under the control of the Education Acts by deeming them to be resident in the place of registration of their boat and thus subject to the bye-laws laid down by the education authorities of that place. In practice, boats often had no connection at all with their place of registration. In such cases parents were supposed to obtain a certificate from the education authorities stating that they were satisfied that the child in question was being efficiently educated elsewhere.

The Canal Boats Act of 1884 required the Education Department to report annually to Parliament on the education of canal-boat children but it did not require them or the employers to make any special provision for them. Section 12 of the 1877

23. Boat boys on board Fellows Morton & Clayton boats with a view of Brentford in the background.
Walter Russon / Alan Faulkner Collection

Canal Boats Act stated that a canal company could appropriate funds for the education and maintenance of canal-boat children but, as there was no obligation placed on them to do so, most canal companies did no more than make the occasional contribution to the efforts of voluntary missions.

The Shropshire Union Company, which had its own carrying department, was to some extent, an exception. From the late nineteenth century, the directors encouraged children living on their boats to attend school by issuing them with attendance record books and requiring company agents to keep the company informed of the number of children attending school and the reasons for any absences.[128] In 1930, the Grand Union Canal Company was persuaded to provide the London City Mission with a barge and to pay for it to be refitted as a floating school.[129] The Canal Boats Bill of 1929–30, which sought to ban children from living on canal boats, mainly on educational grounds, was going through Parliament at this time and it seems to have been a fear that such a ban would ruin the industry that spurred the Canal Company into this belated show of concern for the welfare of boat children.

Although the last quarter of the nineteenth century saw canal-boat children officially brought under the regulation of the Education Acts, the provisions of the Canal Boats Acts concerning schooling were very easily evaded by those who wished to do so and did nothing to help those parents who would have liked to see their children educated. Most local education authorities felt that nothing could be done to secure even a basic education for these children until there was a change in the law to prohibit them from living on board. During 1917, articles appeared in the press and Cheshire County Council urged the Board of Education to consider canal-boat children in the new Education Bill, yet the Fisher Education Act of 1918 was allowed to pass into law without a single provision to help these children.

In June of 1919, Sir Edmund Phipps of the Board of Education wrote in a minute to one of his civil servants:

Mr Richards and I are feeling unhappier than ever about the children on canal boats. We have some reports which are not pleasant reading and we are wondering if you have any papers which will show how far this subject was considered when the Education Bill of last year was being prepared. I have a vague recollection of being consulted and of saying that it still seemed to us to be a hopeless problem.[130]

The reply came the next day:

I am almost sure that there are no papers of any use in

connection with canal boat children and the Education Bill. I believe the point was mentioned on various occasions in the course of the discussions of the Bill and that the view taken was that compulsory boarding out of canal boat children was the only possible method of solving the educational difficulties. It was felt, however, that any proposal to remove children compulsorily from the control of their parents would give rise to strong objection, and in view of the other controversial matters in the Bill I do not think the project was seriously examined.

Between 1919 and 1930, the transport unions campaigned to improve the lot of families living on board canal boats. This campaign gave rise to a Ministry of Health Committee of Enquiry into the practice of living-in and finally to a Private Member's Bill which was introduced by Harry Gosling in 1929. The Committee had recommended that children of school age should be banned from living on boats, at least during term time, and the Bill

sought to make this law. It failed ultimately, and although the campaign did result in a great deal of attention being paid to canal-boat children during the 1920s, there were no resulting changes in the law which might have assisted in securing them a basic education.[131]

Under section 39(iii) of the 1944 Education Act, special provision was made whereby children whose parents were engaged in any trade or business which required them to travel from place to place were required to make at least 200 attendances at school per year. During 1944, meetings were held between the Board of Education, the Ministry of War Transport and the National Association of Canal Carriers to see how boat people could be helped to meet the requirements of the new Act.[132] This resulted in little change to the way of life of those families remaining on the boats. A children's hostel was opened in Erdington, Birmingham in 1952. It was

24. A child on board *Cardonia* at Hatten Locks. *National Waterways Museum*

run by the Birmingham Education Authority and housed up to thirty children who could then attend Birches Green School. *Waterways,* the staff magazine of British Transport Waterways reported that by 1958 about 100 children had passed through the hostel but it added that:

… when they leave school at fifteen, the canals call to them. It is in their blood and most of them go back to the life they were born to.

Despite the good work of this hostel, there were many more children who remained on the boats throughout the 1950s and 60s where the problem of school attendance remained as great and the law as ineffective as ever.

Canal-boat children and the ordinary elementary schools

CHILDREN who travelled from place to place on boats were expected to attend the ordinary elementary schools in whichever place they found themselves. In practice this proved to be very difficult for both educational and social reasons. As educational standards amongst other working-class children improved, it became increasingly difficult to assimilate boat children into the ordinary classes. Because of their infrequent attendance and lack of continuity, their attainments were poor and many schools regarded them as burdensome transients who had merely to be kept occupied for the short period of their attendance and prevented from extending an undesirable influence over the other children. Boat people, and their children, had a reputation for using strong language and in 1918, one Birmingham schoolmaster claimed that a boat boy could 'corrupt' a school of 400 in half a day![133] Selina Dix, the headteacher of Wheatley Street School, Coventry told the Committee on Living-in in 1920:

The canal children are always placed near my desk and kept under close observation. Their standard of morality is lower than that of normal schoolgirls … They are very careless about the language they use.[134]

One has to sympathise with the teachers who were obliged to deal with these children on a casual basis. A school inspector reporting on the educational attainments of boat children in Cheshire in 1926 found that amongst a number of nine-year-old boat children he tested, the average ability in addition and subtraction was equivalent to a child of six years and five months and the average reading age was five years and seven months.[135] It is not surprising that in some schools they were given nothing but handicrafts or copying to do or were placed in the infant class. This extract from an article in *The Schoolmaster* for 17 May 1919 underlines the difficulty of accommodating children who attended school so irregularly:

The Local Education Authority of the registration town bestows an 'attendance book' upon every child of school age found on the registered boat and admonishes parents to obey the law. These attendance books are marvellous records of wonderful irregularity. 'Sarah M', aged twelve cannot read or write. She never will. During the year 1918 she made one attendance at B, in March three attendances at C, and one at W; in April she went twice to the school at B, and was then continuously absent, and continuously employed in the extremely laborious tasks of loading and unloading, of tramping weary miles leading the horse, of opening locks. In October, Sarah went to school at B for a day, for a half a day at C and made two attendances at W. Surely such records (and they are plentiful) but mock the law as the parents spurn the authority that cannot enforce it. The teacher is required to state 'standard child worked in'. In what standard could Sarah be placed?

The difficulty of knowing in which Standard to place boat children is born out in HMI Dakin's report of 1926[136] in which he noted 'an undesirable tendency' in some teachers 'to group them, regardless of age, in the same class, generally a junior one'. Not only were they placed in classes well below the age-group of their peers but there was little consistency between one school and another. Dakin found one child who had been placed in Standard I at one school but was placed in Standard IV in another. He felt that:

Even though these children [were] not equal in attainments with children of their own age in higher classes, there [was] much that they would learn unconsciously by being in touch with them.

Dr Donald Fraser, Clerk to the Runcorn Education Sub-committee agreed, telling the Committee on Living-in that:

Failing a Special Class, it would seem desirable, in the case of children who rarely attend, to place them among children of their own age; the social contact in school and playground would probably be more beneficial than a small amount of information picked up among smaller children, association with whom would not conduce to increasing their self-respect or be for the good of the young children themselves.[137]

Not only education officials felt that the way some schools treated boat children was wrong. The boat people themselves had their objections. Dr Wilson from the Ministry of Health spoke to a Mrs Ball on the boat *Dawley* in 1930:

Mrs Ball is keen on school education for her children but has definite views on method. She objected when she found her children at the Birmingham school sitting on a clean floor engaged in handwork occupations. 'Put 'em in desks and learn 'em as you would your own' was her firm command to the teacher. Mrs Ball re-inspected the school a fortnight later and was satisfied as the children were then sitting in desks![138]

William Bagnall, a boatman, reported in 1920 that there was a school at Ellesmere Port where:

… they were more 'struck' on the children; they used to make them do things; if a child went there, they would make it understand what it was doing; they would not turn it out half learned; they would make it take notice of what it had to do.[139]

Unfortunately, boat children were not well received at most ordinary schools. As HMI Ball pointed out:

… the school can do practically nothing for such a child. If he is a normal boy he will not find his bearings in under a week when it is time to move on and his teacher knows only too well that it is no use giving him special attention. He is a not too welcome visitor … [boat children] don't like going to the ordinary schools at their outports and they pretty successfully avoid them as a rule. It is safe to say that even if they go to school at the outport they get practically nothing from it.[140]

NAME	BORN	STANDARD	ATTENDANCES			REMARKS
			1916/17 possible 299	1917/18 416	1918/19 399	
BIRCH John	2.9.06	I	27	24	60	Well-developed boy with plenty of brains who would have made good progress if regular attendance had been possible. Has not entered school this year. Totally unable to read and can only do copy writing. Quite unable to write a simple sentence or his name. Attendances this year 0.
SPIERS William	14.10.05	II	58	44	14	Just taken off register having reached 14 yrs. Boy with plenty of brain power who owing to shocking attendance only just reached Std II. Before entering school at age 7 had been badly kicked by a horse he was driving and bears the scar on his forehead. Attendances this term 1.
SPIERS Fred	23.3.08	I	132	77	104	Irregularity alone has been the cause of this boy, at age 11, being in Std I. Can read infant reader with assistance and can write his name but has no idea of writing a sentence. Attendances this term 13.
STOKES John	14.12.11	IB	126			Has been on the books for a year but owing to terrible irregularity cannot read or write, does not know letters. Father, mother, two girls (one over 14) and John used to go on the boat. Youngest girl now in infirmary with injured hand so mother remains in Gloucester but little John is still taken on boat. Attendances this term 4.

TABLE 4. Extract from the Register of Canal Boat Boys, Archdeacon Council School (Source: Board of Education File PRO ED 11/88)

One would not be surprised to hear the comments of several boat children who, when talking to HMI Chambers of their dislike of attending ordinary schools, said that 'the house children gives us looks … they spits at us … they calls us names'.[141] (Oddly, Chambers thought that there was little real basis for these remarks. Surely few people who work regularly with school children would agree!) However, the boat children were apparently the victims of appalling ignorance and prejudice on the part of some of the teachers. When Selina Dix was asked by the Committee on Living-in whether she thought that boat children were 'under-fed', she replied:

I do not think the children are under-fed. Some of them are very small for their age, but I do not think it is due to under-feeding. I think that their skins are not as stretchable as those of ordinary children, because they are under-bathed.[142]

As indicated earlier, it was not only the children who had no other home but the boat who suffered in their schooling. In Gloucester, most boat families had houses in the town in which part of the family lived but still the boys, and sometimes the girls, were taken away from school from an early age to help on the boats. TABLE 4 shows a few extracts from the register of boat boys at Archdeacon Street Council School along with the comments of the teacher. The register contains many more pages of names, all with similar comments.

In Runcorn in 1920, the Education Sub-committee reported that there were thirty-three boat children on the books of Runcorn schools in that year. Of these, thirty had homes ashore but their mothers and fathers still went away with the boats, only using their houses when in the neighbourhood.[143] The children, therefore, still had the same problems when it came to schooling.

Special schools for canal-boat children

As indicated before, the earliest schools specially for canal-boat children were Sunday schools in Manchester and Runcorn and a day school in Oxford, all of which were established before 1841. Unfortunately almost nothing is known about these schools and little more about the class for boat children held on Worcester Wharf, Birmingham

since about 1857. The latter was run by a missionary organisation called the Incorporated Seamen and Boatmen's Friend Society. The 'Boatmen's Hall', run by this society opened on the wharf in March 1879 on land donated by the canal company. It was later demolished because of road works, and a new building was opened in 1885. The Boatmen's Hall here and another one at Birchalls still operated as community and missionary centres until after the Second World War but the school closed in 1893 and boat children had to attend the local elementary school.[144]

In Brentford, the London City Mission started a school for canal-boat children in about 1896. By 1900 there were said to be 500 children on the register although the number of children present on any particular day varied between fifty and none. Teaching was undertaken by the Missonary's daughter with the Missionary himself coming in from time to time to play the harmonium and hold hymn practices. An article in the *Morning Leader* of 3 March 1900 gave an account of a visit to the school made by one of their journalists. In language very different from the politically correct 'journalese' of today, the writer described the twenty children in attendance on that particular day in the following terms:

Their ages were from three or four to fourteen or fifteen. They were evidently of widely different degrees of intelligence. One had the brightest, most taking face, his neighbour had the narrow forehead, dull eyes and heavy lips indicative of a low order, not only of intelligence but also of humanity. Another, bright enough in appearance gave his teacher perpetual trouble by swearing. Well, poor boy, too often he heard bad language all day long. The colour of another boy's face remained one of a certain classic advertisement for Pears' Soap; but in the form next to him sat three of the neatest, cleanest little girls anyone could wish to see.

The writer went on to describe the children's copy-books, kept on the mantelpiece while they were away on the boats. The children were taught reading, writing, arithmetic, a little geography and simple Bible stories. The journalist talked with the children and tried to find out how much they had gleaned from their lessons:

Almost all the most familiar English wild birds were named – finches, larks, pee-wits etc. Nobody had seen the sea but somebody knew what a seagull was. Somebody else was very proud of knowing about an eagle. With animals we managed quite as well, but the first names called out were not those of animals which the children had ever seen. Brought up almost entirely in the country, they had never heard of the zoo. Yet 'elephant', 'lion', 'tiger' and 'camel' came very quickly, but nobody could tell me what a kangaroo or a hippopotamus was. Sometimes, too, it was hard to recognize the animals under the quaint country names the children had given them.

If we went to London and took a train to Dover and then sailed straight across the sea, what country would we come to?

This was too hard. Nobody knew anything about Dover, although they knew of all sorts of little out-of-the-way almost unknown inland places in 'the shires'. Nobody had any idea what country lay on the other side of the channel though a good many had heard the name of France.

What names of towns did they know? Oh, a great many, from 'Brummegem' downstairs. 'Birmingham' they would hardly have heard of. Did anybody know what was the biggest town in England? – in all the world? 'Heaven!' was the prompt answer. 'Heaven is not in the world', I had to tell them. 'Not yet.' But eventually it was decided that London was the biggest.

The article reported that a new and larger school was soon to be built but a few years later the canal-boat school was closed. It reopened in 1920 in a small hall in the London City Mission's Boatmen's Institute at The Butts, Brentford. The school was now run by the Local Education Authority who rented the hall for £25 per annum. Miss Baker, a teacher from the nearby Rothschild Council School, was put in charge and her salary was increased from £235 to £255.[145] The Board of Education later frowned on this move as the teacher became a quasi headmistress and it was found impossible to 'demote' her and redeploy her as an ordinary teacher in another school.

At first the class was held in the mornings only but this was later extended to cover afternoons also. The school was popular but boats came into the depot at any time and so it was not possible for children to keep regular school hours. When the school was inspected in February 1920,[146] fifty-three children had been admitted although there was only one boy present on the day of the

25. Boatmen's floating chapel at Oxford, 1851.
Railway & Canal Historical Society Collection

26. The Boatmen's Institute, Brentford, opened 13 December 1904.
Alan Faulkner Collection

inspection. The room could accommodate up to twenty children but the average class size was said to be seven. Lighting, heating and ventilation were all found to be satisfactory. There were ten tables and twenty chairs, only one lavatory for both boys and girls and no latrines or wash basins. The Butts, which it was supposed had once been a village green, afforded ample open space for games etc.

By January 1928 there were 350 children on the register. Miss Baker reported enthusiastically that:

No difficulty has been experienced here in drawing these little 'bargees' to school. They return at the end of their trip often before the boat is made fast, running in with renewed zest for mastering the knowledge of which their parents, in most cases are totally deficient.

Much pride is taken in their homework books and work done on the journey abroad proudly displayed. The school 'library' affords much joy to its 'readers.[147]

Despite the popularity of the school, the itinerant way of life of the boat families meant that the children could make few attendances. Miss Baker reported in that same year that only eight children had made as many as 100 attendances out of 428 possible. 51 children had attended between 50 and 100 times and a further 20 had made 40 or 50 attendances.

When the school was inspected in October 1930

by HMI Chambers,[148] he reported that the accommodation was poor. He felt that a nominal roll of 364 children was too great a burden for one teacher and a fifteen-year-old monitress. He felt that the general standard of attainments at Brentford was very low, worse than at the other special school at Paddington, although he acknowledged that in both schools the work was being conducted with 'a high degree of earnestness and ability'. Unlike the Paddington school, the Brentford Canal Boat Class had become entirely separated from the parent school, Rothschild, and the headteacher there no longer felt any responsibility for the instruction at the Boatmen's Institute.

If the education received at the school was necessarily meagre, at least some of the children were given the opportunity of obtaining medical treatment which they might not otherwise have done. When a Ministry of Health doctor visited the school in 1930[149] she was able to report that the school nurse made weekly visits to the class and made follow-up visits to the boats to urge parents to obtain treatment for their children where necessary.

With the failure of the Private Member's Bill in 1930, the attention of the Board of Education turned away from canal-boat children and little more is heard of the special schools. The Chiswick

27. Mr Chapman from the Boatman's Mission, Brentford standing on *Gardenia.*
Alan Faulkner Collection

Canal Boat Inspector reported in 1943[150] that the Brentford School was still operating with an average class size of nine. The school was visited again in November 1943[151] by a Ministry of Health official who described the accommodation which consisted of two large rooms. One was used as a class room and was furnished with desks and a blackboard; the other was used as a playroom. By February 1945[152] the school was closed and the building was being used as a store for furniture from bombed houses. The children were thought to attend the local elementary school on Boston Manor Road. It reopened in March of 1946 but thereafter its history remains obscure.

At Paddington, a special school for boat children was opened in 1926 in the headquarters of the Church Army Mission. By 1930 there were two classes operating under the supervision of the headteacher of St Michael's School, Star Street.

Unlike the parent school at Brentford, the head-teacher of St Michael's was said to take a close interest in the work of the boat children.[153] During these years there were around 100 children on roll with class sizes averaging about nine. The London County Council Education Committee reported in 1930 that, considering the difficulties, the attainments of the children were reasonably good, especially in handwork in which they were keenly interested. Reading was still a particular difficulty as the children lacked the opportunity for regular practice but, once it was mastered, children were given homework to take with them on their journeys.

The school was visited in 1930[154] by Susan Lawrence MP, the Parliamentary Secretary to the Ministry of Health. She made the following notes on what she saw:

I saw the school. Roll 97. Attendance 18. Very bad

28. *Evelyn* at Paddington, almost certainly at the dedication of the school barge *Elsdale* in 1930.
Alan Faulkner Collection

building. A teacher lent by L.C.C., apparently one of our good average teachers. The top class 11 –13, about eight children, were learning out of a First Reader. A girl of thirteen couldn't read at all – a girl of eleven read about as well as a child of eight – a big boy (about twelve) was spelling out his words and did the 'backward trick' you meet with in little children – 'saw' for 'was'.

They said attendance was bad – the other day they had twenty six. The school register was a curiosity – pages of 0 with the occasional mark for present. Physical appearance about on a level with comparable neighbouring bad schools – much like Conway Street.

Wharfs really disgusting. Open barges loaded with crude refuse … Sorting of refuse and pressing of tins carried out in a rough primitive sort of way … Saw some barges with little children. Those I saw made a very bad impression on me – by eye, the worst type of slum child. Cabins incredibly cramped … Women were jolly creatures – very independent – not pleased to see us – rather like Covent Garden porters – never saw women I should better like to organise.

Later in 1930, the premises in which the school was held were demolished to make way for an extension to St Mary's Hospital. An appeal by the Bishop of London in a letter to *The Times* managed to raise funds for a new school and the Grand Union Canal Company provided a large warehouse on the dockside. The new premises were said to be an improvement on the old but later in the 1930s the Paddington school closed due to poor attendance.[155]

Harry Gosling's Bill aroused much controversy over the rearing and education of canal-boat children. The carrying companies were worried that if children left the boats their mothers would follow. A good source of cheap labour would be lost and the next generation of boat people would be denied their initial training. Fears about this no doubt motivated the Grand Union Canal Company to

49

provide the warehouse accommodation for the school at Paddington. In the same year they also provided a barge which was refitted as a school and towed to Otter Wharf, Horton Road, West Drayton. The school opened in October 1930 and the Middlesex Education Committee described the accommodation to the Board of Education in the following terms:

The school is conducted in a reconditioned barge. The superficial area of the classroom is about 240 square feet. There are two radiators heated from an 'Ideal' domestic heater installed in the stern of the barge. The room is fairly well ventilated and the lighting is good. The only means of artificial lighting is an incandescent lamp. There is a small staff room which opens out of the classroom. On the opposite side of this room, about twenty one pegs have been affixed to the wooden partition of the corridor. This is the only cloakroom accommodation. The sanitary accommodation consists of a small office with a chemical closet, the contents of which are removed each evening by the caretaker.

There is a small area in front of the classroom which could be used as an open air classroom in fine weather.

There is no free space on the wharf off which the barge is moored so that no playground area is available ashore, nor is there any space on which temporary accommodation could be erected.[156]

The school was taken over by the Local Authority within a year of it opening and attached to a local elementary school. In 1939 the barge itself sank but the school was re-established on the bank at Bulls Bridge which was one of the main depots for the Grand Union Canal Carrying Company. In 1956 the school was moved to new premises yet again. A large classroom at Norwood Green Infants' School was given over to canal-boat children and they were ferried to and from the canal by car. The move enabled children to enjoy games on the school field and join with the other children at playtime. School dinners were served to canal-boat children in their own separate room. This was also used as a play-room and contained toys, games, a large doll's house and two camp-beds with pillows and blankets for children who were not feeling well.[157]

After Easter 1958, the appointment of another teacher enabled the school to remain open to boat children on six days per week and during the school holidays, closing for only two weeks in August and on Bank Holidays. It was hoped that a hostel would be built at Bulls Bridge to enable the children to attend more regularly but this never came about. The special class at Norwood Green finally closed in December 1962.

29. Interior of the barge school *Elsdale*.
National Waterways Museum

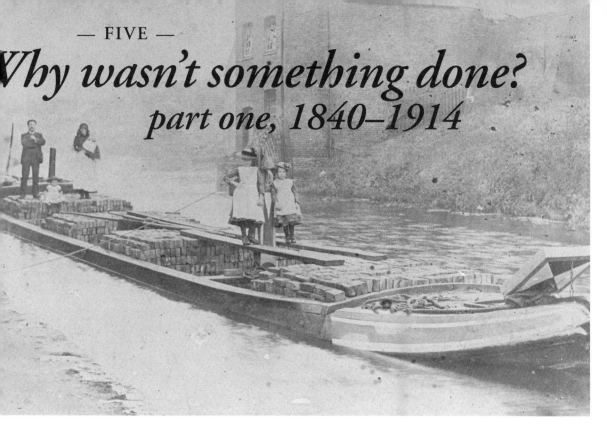

— FIVE —
Why wasn't something done?
part one, 1840–1914

IT HAS been shown in chapter two that, although canal-boat people were not wealthy, the majority were not badly paid. Those in regular work, especially those working for a big carrier, would have enjoyed a standard of income which compared favourably with other manual workers of the day. Yet there was much about the lives of families living permanently or semi-permanently on the boats which might have given cause for concern to social reformers; the cramped living space, the lack of sanitary facilities, the neglect of children's education and the absence of any regulations controlling hours, conditions of work and the employment of children, young persons and women.

As the nineteenth century wore on, more and more people, and their places of work, were brought

under the control of some sort of legislation which was aimed at alleviating the worst effects of industrialisation and urbanisation. Some Victorian employers were noted for their paternalism and philanthropy and the voluntary sector, particularly non-conformist missionary societies, turned their attention towards relieving the suffering and misery of the most impoverished sections of society. In factories, mines and workshops, and even in the fields, the conditions under which women and children laboured had attracted most attention. One might reasonably expect, therefore, in that age of increasing state intervention and concern for human welfare, that something would have been done to improve life for the women and children of the cut.

In fact, modern historians[158] have argued that, far from being an age of philanthropy, the nineteenth century saw the continued existence of widespread callousness and indifference to the suffering of others, especially among employers. There was, it seems, no general agreement about what consti-

---

30 (*above*). The Halford family aboard a wide boat above Copper Mill Lock, Harefield *c*.1895.
W. T. Herridge / Alan Faulkner Collection

tuted intolerable conditions and no guarantee that 'intolerability' would bring about a remedy. Christianity, commonly held to be the motivating force behind social reform, often had the opposite effect with the church acting as a barrier to social change and even opposing the alleviation of suffering on the grounds that misery was a test ordained by God.

At the beginning of the nineteenth century, the predominant middle- and upper-class view of poverty and social distress was that these were necessary evils and that without hunger men would become idle. Many of those social reformers who considered themselves humanitarians were, in fact, merely moralists, concerned not so much with the hardships and sufferings of the poor but with their immorality.

Sunday working

CONCERN about the moral standing of the boat people led to the appointment of a House of Lords Select Committee in 1841 to enquire whether canal carriers should be allowed to operate on a Sunday, thus denying their employees the opportunity of attending church.

It is clear from the evidence taken by the Committee that contemporaries saw the effects of moral instruction as having clear connections with physical and social well-being. Several of the witnesses described some sections of the boat population as 'demoralised' (not in the modern sense but meaning immoral or amoral) and 'degraded' and the clergyman at the Boatmen's Bethel in Oxford was said to have 'never seen anything to equal the dreadful State they [the boatmen] were in'. This he attributed to their 'want of little education' and 'want of proper moral and religious training'. Such degradation was said to lead to profanity, profligacy and drunkenness, this latter vice in particular being held responsible for the descent into poverty, wretchedness and criminality. It is clear from the exchanges between Committee members and witnesses that both sides believed the relief of such social evils would come, not from voluntary provision nor from the state, but from the moral improvement of the individuals concerned which would enable them to exercise the self-discipline and self-help for which the Victorian age has come to be known.[159]

There was no question that the state should provide for the needs of the workforce nor bear any part of the cost of such provision. The duty of the state was merely to legislate in order to compel employers to do so. With this in mind, there was much concern on the part of the Committee with the effect on canal carrying that a mandatory Sunday stoppage would have. In many places, Sunday was the busiest day of the week on the canals. Manufacturers, getting off to a slow start at the beginning of the week, hurried to get their products finished by Saturday. The canal boats would be loaded on Saturday night and ready to go by Sunday morning. If the canals were to be closed until Monday it was feared that this would drive even more trade onto the railways at a time when canals were already being badly affected by this new rival. This view seems to have weighed most heavily with their Lordships, despite the fact that several carriers already prohibited the movement of boats on Sunday.

The result was that the evidence of the enquiry was submitted without report, observation or recommendation and no action on the matter was ever taken.

George Smith of Coalville and the Canal Boat Acts

IN 1873, an obscure Methodist 'enthusiast' turned social reformer, opened his campaign on behalf of the women and children of the canals. George Smith was born in 1831, the son of a Staffordshire brick-maker.[160] He was said to have received a little formal education at the hands of a Primitive Methodist but, as he began work in the brickyards at the age of seven, he was mainly self-educated. Inspired by a peculiarly extreme brand of religious motivation – it was said that even his friends could not take both the man and his enthusiasm – Smith believed himself to be 'marked out by Divine Providence for special work'. This he began in 1871 on behalf of the children who worked in the brickyards and his agitations resulted in the passage of the Factory (Brick and Tile Yard Extension) Act later the same year.

In October 1873, he turned his attention to the canal-boat population. Motivated by his Christian

31. Family boats at Trent Lock.
Alan Faulkner Collection

faith, the supposed immorality of the boat people was Smith's main concern. Their lack of religious instruction, their foul language, coarse manners, drunkenness and the fact that they were said to live together as man and wife outside marriage, caused him much anxiety, but he also drew attention to their insanitary accommodation, the harshness of their labours and the labouring of their children.[161]

Smith's agitation led the Factory and Workshop Acts Commission in 1875 to turn its attention to canal-boat labour. Some supplementary questions for inspectors asking the extent to which women and children were employed on boats and what provision was made for the children's education, were included in an appendix. Some witnesses were also examined on this issue and on this occasion, in addition to the canal proprietors and clergy, one actual boatman and a former boatman were examined.[162] Although reference was still made to the morals of the boat people, the commissioners seemed to be primarily concerned with the reality of social conditions on the canals. They asked about child labour and education, about the organisation of the trade and the need for family labour; they asked about the men's wages and provision for seasonal unemployment, the size of the cabin accommodation and about health, diet and sanitary conditions.

The contrast between this and the tone of the 1841 enquiry is quite marked, yet the reference to 'decency' and 'respectability' indicate the persistence of the distinction between the 'deserving' and the 'undeserving' poor which characterised much of the nineteenth-century attitude to social policy from the 1834 Poor Law reforms onwards.

One of the problems which reformers faced was that the only way in which social conditions could really be improved for boat families was for children, and perhaps women also, to be banned from the boats. Yet it seemed that if such a prohibition were to be brought about by law, it would go against one of the main aims of social legislation in the period, which was to inculcate such norms as respectability and family cohesion.

Smith wanted to see children removed from the supposed demoralising influence of the overcrowded and insanitary boat cabins. Others felt that if the women and children were forced to live on shore, immorality would increase since, as the Reverend Dr Bell put it, 'you do not know what the husbands may be doing, and you do not know what the wives may be doing at home'.[163] This latter position was maintained by canal-boat missionaries throughout the history of family labour on canal boats. It led the Incorporated Seamen and Boatmen's Friend Society and the London City Mission to oppose any proposal to remove children from canal boats, even in the mid-twentieth century. They preferred instead to provide special canal-side facilities to meet the social and spiritual needs of the boating population.

The Factory Commissioners in their report of 1876 felt that canal-boat work was so far removed from anything like the work of a factory or workshop that it could not be included in an extension to the existing factory legislation. They did feel, however, that the social deprivation of the boating population merited government intervention. They recommended that children over three years of age and young females be excluded from the boats but their recommendations were not taken up.

Smith continued to urge reform. He called for a prohibition of boys under thirteen and girls under eighteen, and regulations for the registering of boats with stipulations as to the minimum cubic feet of air space required in the cabin, the number, age and sex of the occupants and the requirement for canal-boat children to reach a certain standard of education before being allowed to take up employment.[164]

Gradually, he began to succeed in interesting others in his cause. Eventually, in May 1877, a Bill was introduced to provide for the regulation of canal boats used as dwellings. The Act was passed in August 1877 and became law the following year. Regulations drawn up under the Act laid down a minimum standard of accommodation on board, and regulated the number, age, and sex of persons permitted to inhabit the cabin. There was nothing, however, to prohibit or limit child labour or to ensure even a minimum of education for children resident on board. Furthermore, there was no provision in the Act for its enforcement. No inspectorate was created and no penalties fixed for violation of its provisions. Implementation was left to local authorities and they did so with varying degrees of enthusiasm. In Birmingham, the Chief Constable of Police was given the responsibility for registering boats. In other districts it was the local Surveyor or Sanitary Inspector. Some were paid nothing for these extra duties whilst others received anything from a flat rate of £2, £10 or £25, to a rate per boat ranging from 2s 6d to one guinea. In some areas the Nuisance or Sanitary Inspectors were appointed to inspect the boats after registration, usually for no extra pay, but in many places there was no one to perform this duty at all.[165]

Not surprisingly, when Smith returned to the canals a short time after the passing of the Act he found little had changed. Further agitation on his part brought an amendment Bill in 1881 but it was blocked at the second reading by the opposition of the canal companies. A second amendment Bill in 1883 was more successful and the matter was referred to a Select Committee. Smith, in his evidence before the committee complained of continuing immorality (co-habitation of unwed members of the opposite sex) and also of inordinately harsh conditions of employment for children, lack of education, overcrowded cabins and the spread of infectious disease.[166] Despite his concern with the physical needs of the boat people, Smith left the committee in no doubt that, in his opinion, it was in their moral condition that the real need lay. When asked to compare the moral and physical condition of the boat population with that of the same class on land, he replied unhesitatingly that the boat people were the moral inferiors of their shore-bound fellows. When pressed on their physical condition, he was hard put to specify any way in which they were actually inferior, although he predicted that physical weakness would begin to show in future years if their present moral state remained unattended.[167]

His call for the enforcement of the Act by regular inspection was not supported by the President of the Local Government Board, nor indeed by the other witnesses. Nevertheless, the Bill, its more radical clauses excluded, passed into law in August 1884, providing for inspection of canal boats by sanitary authorities under a centrally appointed Chief Canal Boat Inspector. It allowed for penalties to be imposed on violations of the Act, and the regulations drawn up under it defined the class of boats to come under its jurisdiction more precisely and gave regulation-making powers to the Education Department.

The Local Government Board accepted responsibility for the Canal Boat Acts only with extreme reluctance. The first Chief Canal Boat Inspector, John Brydone, a businessman from the salt-manufacturing district of Droitwich, took up his new duties with enthusiasm. This further irritated the officials at the Board. Their attitude can be clearly discerned in the correspondence between the Board and Brydone.[168] They drastically edited his reports and insisted that he confine himself to 'actual facts of inspections'. They discouraged his recommendation for change and improvement in the law and deplored his observations on its shortcomings. They made unreasonable demands about the timing of his reports and refused to make simple common-sense adjustments to their administrative practices which would have helped in this regard. They even made unwarranted incursions into Brydone's private business and addressed him in a tone befitting a junior clerk rather than a senior member of the inspectorate. Gradually, Brydone was alienated from the central administration and his untimely death in 1899 was hardly mourned by the Board.

Owen Llewellyn and the Local Government Board

WITH the death in 1899 of John Brydone, the post of Chief Canal Boat Inspector passed to Owen J. Llewellyn. Llewellyn conformed much more than Brydone to the image of a professional public servant. Whilst he carried out his duties conscientiously, he seems to have distanced himself more from the human aspects of the job and become less emotionally involved than Brydone, who at times seemed to feel he had embarked on a personal crusade to raise boat people out of their social wretchedness. In some of his later reports, Llewellyn noted with satisfaction the increasing departure of the 'old-fashioned type of official' who was being replaced by a 'better, more conscientious and abler class of inspector … one who has been educated to be an inspector … and studied his profession'.[169] No doubt Llewellyn placed himself in this new class of professionals.

There is evidence, however, that even Llewellyn required some degree of re-education before his views conformed to the requirements of the Local Government Board. In his report for 1902–3, he drew attention to the disadvantages attending the regular presence of a large number of women and children on board canal boats and declared that no hardship would result if they were prohibited from residing on board. He repeated this assertion the following year and added that the educational clauses of the Canal Boats Acts were inadequate to the task of ensuring the attendance of canal-boat children at school.

In his report for 1905–6, the contrast in tone and attitude is quite remarkable. Speaking at length on the condition of the canal-boat children he claimed:

… the boat child is morally and physically … superior to the land child in a similar station of life … Its open air life inures it to all weathers and its familiarity with its work from a very early age makes its reliant and strong and brings out its best qualities. The sense of responsibility from early youth which makes the British naval officer the type of a perfect public servant has a similar effect on the boat children in the performance of their work. On the boats, boys and girls (whose contemporaries ashore are, in their hobbledehoyhood, a source of worry and anxiety to their parents) can be found doing their duty in a quiet matter-of-fact way and taking a pride in its successful accomplishment. Undoubtedly, those ashore are more fully equipped in the matter of learning but in the application of it I do not think most of them have any advantage over the boat children.

Remarking that he would have liked to see canal-boat children have educational opportunities more equal to those of other children, he reported that this would have been impossible unless they were prohibited from living on board and his comment 'even if this were desirable' implies that he had now turned against such a prohibition. That such was, in fact, the case is made clear in subsequent reports.

One can only speculate on the cause of this about-face on the part of the Chief Inspector. Perhaps greater familiarity with the canals had persuaded him of the desirability of preserving this traditional way of life but it seems unlikely. His concluding remarks: 'I have written fully on this subject as there seems to be an enormous amount of ignorance, exaggeration and misplaced sympathy now prevalent', suggest that it was a closing of ranks on the part of the Local Government Board in the face of growing criticism and the possibility of having to take direct action to remedy the deteriorating social position of the boating population.

Chester Town Council had, that same year, passed a resolution declaring:

… that in the opinion of this council, life on canal boats is detrimental to the moral, mental and physical development of children and it is desirable that the Canal Boats Acts and Education Acts be amended, prohibiting the use of canal boats as dwelling places for children in order that such children may be brought under the effective operation of the compulsory attendance clauses of the Education Acts.[170]

Other municipal authorities passed similar resolutions in the same year. In February 1905, the Northwich Rural District Council passed a motion prohibiting school-aged children from travelling on boats.[171] It is doubtful whether they had the legal power to actually do this and certain that they found it impossible to put into action. The mover of the motion, J. A. Johnson, stated in a report forwarded to the Board of Education that he considered the education of the canal-boat children to be 'a farce'.

Referring to Llewellyn's estimate in his annual report for 1904, that there would not be more than 400 children with no other home than the boat, he commented:

My point is that though a man had a home, he takes his wife and children with him on the boat.

I therefore cannot accept Mr Llewellyn's statement when he infers that there are only 400 boat children in England and Wales who have no other home than the boat and that, therefore, it is only these children who do not go to school. I think it would be more correct to say that most of the 7,000 boats used as dwellings take children with them, if not always, very often. I can state from my own observation of five years on the banks of the canal at Lostock, that there are children on nearly every boat that passes our works.

There is little doubt that Llewellyn's change of heart was provoked by these attacks. The following year, he was still condemning the 'great deal of misplaced sympathy and exaggeration … [which] still exists in various places on the subject of the occupation by children of canal boats'.[172]

Certainly his own sympathies were never thus misplaced again. In the same report his assertion that boat children 'are superior [to land children], and grow up to be better citizens by reason of their training to face hard work and to fight life's bitter battles on their own account', shows that ideas of social justice and social rights were still unknown to some government officials.

An opportunity to bring about the legislation necessary to improve conditions for canal-boat children did present itself around this time with the introduction of the Bill leading to the Children's Act of 1908. Section 118 of this Act provided that a person habitually wandering from place to place and taking with him any child above the age of five years old, must provide for the proper attendance of such a child at school. Defaulters could be fined and the children sent to industrial school. However, canal-boat children were specifically excluded from this provision on the grounds that the Canal Boats Acts already provided for their education.

Richard Parr of the NSPCC, in his book on canal-boat children published in 1910, claimed that a strong plea had been made to include clauses relating to canal-boat children in this Act but the attempt had run into difficulties owing to the fact that the Bill was in the hands of the Home Office

32. Families on boats at Long Buckby.
Alan Faulkner Collection

who had no responsibility for canals.[173] Probably of greater significance was the attitude of the Local Government Board who apparently had no desire to see such a measure brought in. In his next report, that of 1907–8, Llewellyn declared:

My views with regard to the presence of children on the boats have undergone no change, and I rejoice to see that the Children's Bill, which has been brought in by the Parliamentary Secretary for Home Affairs, will not operate to exclude them from the surroundings of their hereditary calling and the good effects of never-ceasing parental supervision.

Around this period, apathy seems to have turned to complacency at the Board. In its report for 1909–10, it declared itself gratified to note that 'the condition of the children is not unsatisfactory from either an educational or a moral point of view'.

It is noticeable that the reports of the Chief Canal Boat Inspector were becoming shorter and more stereotyped during this period. Indeed, his reports for 1910–11 and 1911–12 are almost exact reproductions of his report for 1909–10 with only the figures updated.

The Board of Education

THE Board of Education seems to have been less complacent about the condition of the boat children but no more willing to act on its behalf.

In June 1887, the Department of Education (from 1899, the Board of Education) began to circulate its inspectors asking them to report on the availability of educational facilities for canal-boat children and the attendance of such children. Circulars were sent out in 1887, 1891, 1893, 1905 and thence annually. Despite some optimistic reports from the Birmingham School Board in the early years,[174] many authorities complained year after year that the difficulties of enforcing the attendance of canal-boat children at school were such that they had more or less abandoned the attempt.

In August 1883, HMI Turnbull complained to the Department:

So long as the child lives on the boat and moves about with the boat, he must have a poor chance of getting anything like a proper education. Inquiry will not remedy this. Legislation, properly enforced is the right remedy.[175]

33. A girl leading a pair of horse-drawn boats at the south end of Braunston Tunnel.
Railway & Canal Historical Society Collection

Seven years later he was still making the same complaint:

As you will doubtless recollect, the Board have more than once memorialised the Department, praying their Lordships to make it illegal for children of school age to dwell on boats but as yet no action has been taken in that direction.[176]

Such pleas did not fall on completely deaf ears. Year after year, from 1900 to 1914, the Board complained in its annual report of the difficulty of enforcing the school attendance of canal-boat children, and of the inadequacy of the present law and it continually affirmed its belief that children should be prohibited from living on board boats. Yet, clearly, it believed that to bring about such a prohibition lay outside its jurisdiction.

This, and the failure to bring canal-boat children under the jurisdiction of the Children's Act of 1908, highlight one of the difficulties which frustrated attempts to reform social conditions on the canals throughout the twentieth century. The Local Government Board and, from 1919, the Ministry of Health, had been given the responsibility of canal-boat supervision. Education was the responsibility of the Board of Education but, because the Canal Boats Acts included educational clauses, there was some overlap of interests. Furthermore, the Board of Trade and, later, the Ministry of Transport and the Ministry of Labour were also involved with some aspects of canal life. This multiplicity of departmental responsibilities, some overlapping, with ill-defined borders, and poor inter-departmental co-operation led to confusion and gave some departments, who were in any case inclined to do little, the excuse to avoid getting involved with reform.

The degree to which central departments began to lose touch, not only with the reality of life on the canals, but also with the experience of each other, is demonstrated in 1904–5 when, in his annual report, Llewellyn stated that the number of women and children living on board was unaltered while the Board of Education in its annual report for the same year remarked:

It is, however, satisfactory to find that, in most districts, it is becoming unusual for either women or children to live permanently on the boats.

Criticism of conditions on the canals and the ineffectiveness of current legislation had been reaching the Board of Education for some years, but in 1906, the year of Llewellyn's change of outlook, it reached something of a climax. In that year, the Assistant Medical Officer of Health for Birmingham wrote a lengthy report on the conditions under which canal-boat children were reared in his district in which he condemned the current legislation for not enforcing adequate standards of space and ventilation in boat cabins.[177] He commented favourably on the cleanliness of the cabins and the health of the occupants but criticised the lack of privacy in the living quarters which he felt led to immorality, immodesty and the neglect of personal cleanliness. His most depressing observations were on the education of the children and their future prospects:

Parents almost invariably stated as a result of enquiry that their children would follow their lives on the canals. Such was almost the only prospect before them and the parents desired nothing better … hence their training in the management of canal boats was considered of greater importance than schooling.

In his concluding remarks he stated:

There is no doubt that the Canal Boat Acts, properly enforced, have greatly altered for the better during the last twenty years, the conditions of life on the canals for both adults and children, but it is quite evident that further powers are necessary before this section of the community can benefit equally with others in the advantages offered by modern legislation. It seems that nothing short of compulsory legal measures keeping the children during school ages either entirely off the boats, or at least for a good part of each year, will enable the canal boat population to come into line with the rest of our industrial community.

The Compulsory Education Act seems to be almost a dead letter so far as it applies to canal boat children and this remedy, while making it impossible for such a state of things to exist, would give opportunities for amending in almost every other way the moral and social condition of no inconsiderable section of our industrial population.

These sentiments were endorsed by James Broscomb, District Inspector of Schools for the City of Birmingham Education Committee who added:

The educational condition of these children is deplorable. With few exceptions they cannot read the simplest book used in an ordinary infants school; they cannot write, their knowledge of numbers is meagre and a good many do not know the value of coins except bronze …

The educational opportunities of these children are few; if every opportunity were taken advantage of, they could not learn much ... The only hope for them in my opinion is by legislation in the direction of making them live ashore.[178]

This swingeing attack produced no noticeable effect at the Board of Education whose annual paragraph relating to canal-boat children became harder and harder to distinguish from that of the previous year.

Several problems lay in the way of reform. Firstly, there was the difficulty of defining clearly where the responsibility for these children lay as far as the central administration was concerned. Secondly, there was the fact that school provision and attendance was clearly the responsibility of the local authority but, in the case of children who moved about from place to place, local control was impossible in practice, even though the law theoretically made provision for it. This difficulty was recognised by the Board as early as 1902 but their reaction was merely to hope that this would be remedied by the widening of authority of the County Councils under the Act of that year.[179] When this turned out not to be the case, the Board could offer nothing better.

Disappointed by the failure of central government to introduce effective legislation to secure a reasonable education for these children, the NSPCC drafted its own Bill in 1910 which sought to ban all children under the age of fourteen years of age from canal boats. Parr said of the Bill at the time, 'Its provisions are simple and should not arouse any active opposition'.[180] However, the Society was unable to persuade anyone to introduce the Bill until after the First World War and, in the light of subsequent events, Parr's optimism seems ill-founded and even naïve.

Social reform did not begin to touch the women and children of the canals until the last quarter of the nineteenth century which, compared with other areas of society, was late. Having come about, the Canal Boats Acts were heavily criticised, by some who thought they were an unwarranted intrusion into privacy, but mainly by those who felt that they did not go far enough. However, it would be wrong to suppose that they were a total failure, at least in their early years. They went some way to reducing overcrowding and they did set a certain standard of accommodation and sanitation which was enforced by fairly regular inspection. Even critics of the Acts acknowledged that some improvement in the social condition of the boat people had been brought about as a result. More importantly, the condition of a particularly little-known and obscure section of the population was opened up to public view, through the work of the canal-boat inspectors.

However, if the Canal Boats Acts were all very well in the closing years of the nineteenth century, even by the early years of the twentieth century they were no longer adequate for ensuring that boat people were adequately housed and educated. This was becoming increasingly obvious to those whose duties and responsibilities placed them in the position of having to try to make good the deficiencies. Of course, it would be wrong to suggest that boat people were the only section of the population not to benefit fully from the new era of social welfare provision. In the period leading up to the First World War, housing legislation remained ineffective and large sections of the working classes continued to be poorly housed. Most adult males were still untouched by protective legislation and, in 1900, the Board of Education published in its annual report complaints of 'excessive employment of school children' and poor school attendance with many children attending school for the first time at the age of eight, twelve or even thirteen.

The administrative difficulties of regulating a population which continually moved from place to place, particularly for a government which favoured the devolution of power to local authorities, were enormous. Although the Local Government Board did provide a central co-ordinating authority in the form of the Chief Canal Boat Inspector, the Board of Education offered no help in co-ordinating the efforts of local education authorities. The multiplicity of government departments involved, their lack of co-operation with one another, and the tendency to assume or hope that certain responsibilities would rest with someone else, exacerbated the situation. Given the heavy work load of officials during a period when a great deal of new social legislation was coming into force, perhaps it is not surprising that one of the least known and least vociferous sectors of society was given such a low priority.

— SIX —
Why wasn't something done?
part two, 1914–1960

UP UNTIL the First World War, if boat people lived hard lives with poor living and working conditions and little or no education, they were no worse off than many other working people. After the war, however, housing, working conditions, and opportunities for education began to improve for most people whilst for the families on the boats little changed.

The First World War

ONE of the main priorities of the government at the outbreak of the war was to gain control of the most important sectors of industry in order to maximise efficient use of labour and material resources to support the war effort. This resulted in, among other things, immediate control of the railways. Canals were considered to be no longer of sufficient importance and at first were left alone. Railway-owned canals did technically come under government control but this was incidental. By 1917, the railways were severely overburdened but the canal system lay idle and neglected. In an apparent attempt to relieve the situation, the government decided to take control of the inland waterways in March of that year. The real reason behind the decision, however, appears to have been fear of social unrest.

Industrial unrest was a particular feature throughout industry in 1917 and some of the grievances raised affected boat people to an extent, although they had long been accustomed to poor

34 *(above).*
Hood and *Hardy* at Toovey's Mill in May 1956.
E. W. Paget Tomlinson / Alan Faulkner Collection

61

and overcrowded living conditions and long hours. Dilution of labour, a major source of unrest in some industries, was of marginal concern to boat people. There was some attempt to recruit unskilled labour from outside the industry which was resented by traditional boat people[181] but, on the whole, wartime conditions tended to enhance the boatman's status rather than diminish it. Possibly for the first time, the real value of his skills was recognised as it was found to be impossible to replace him with men not born and bred to the trade and, in some areas, experienced men were said to be commanding double wages.[182]

In most places, however, wages did not increase in line with other industries and this gave rise to a great deal of unrest on the canals. Railway companies, with their profits guaranteed by the government, were able to pay war bonuses to their employees whilst independent canal carriers struggled to stay in business with rising running costs and diminishing trade. Finally, with strikes threatened on various waterways and boat owners complaining that they could no longer carry on, the government felt compelled to take control. The canals were brought under the jurisdiction of the Board of Trade with the setting up of a Canal Control Committee which met for the first time on the 28 February 1917.[183] A few months later, the necessity of giving

35. Nellie Fregth on board *Dragonfly* in Hatten Lock.
National Waterways Museum

financial guarantees to the major carrying companies was also accepted.

For the first time in their history, the opportunity was created to run the canals in a fully co-ordinated way, although, as with the railways, the day-to-day running was left to individual companies as before. Nevertheless, government intervention did affect conditions on the canals in some important ways.

For the first time, central control allowed some measure of standardisation on the question of wages and hours. Allied to this was the fact that the Dock, Wharf, Riverside & General Workers' Union was given official recognition and a small part to play in the management of the waterways. Although the union never succeeded in having labour representation on the central Control Committee, three regional sub-committees were set up in June 1917 to which labour representatives were appointed.[184] Although early application by the union on behalf of boatmen for increased wages were ignored by the central committee, later proposals met with more success and by August 1919, all boatmen affected by government control were being paid 33⅓% over pre-war net wages in lieu of a 48-hour week. Canals were closed on Sundays and at night. Proposals for holidays with pay were, however, never agreed by the central body.[185]

The Canal Control Committee was also of some help in relieving other problems facing boat families. When it was reported in February 1918 that boat people were experiencing difficulty obtaining food supplies, the Chairman was able to approach the Food Controller and arrangements were made to issue Travellers' Tickets to boatmen in order to obtain supplies at various points on the canal routes.[186]

August 1919 saw the return of the inland waterways to private ownership. During the period of control, there had been no real attempt to make proper efficient use of the canals and certainly the reorganisation and modernisation of the system – a move which could have solved many of the economic and social problems of the industry – had never been contemplated. Unrest amongst the work-force had been temporarily quelled through war bonuses but nothing really radical was achieved or even attempted.

The most serious social problems affecting canal-boat people, namely education and the use of child and family labour, were completely unaffected and, in fact, actually worsened during the period of the war. One reason for this was that, paradoxically, while central government control increased in some areas of the canal industry, in others it diminished. The Chief Canal Boat Inspector was absent on military service and although local inspectors continued in some places, the Local Government Board had no direct contact with canal-boat administration for the duration of the war and ceased to include any reference to it in its annual report.

The Board of Education continued to receive returns from its local authorities concerning the attendance of canal-boat children. They showed that, if anything, attendance actually declined. In some districts, particularly the West Midlands and South Staffordshire, the number of children residing on canal boats increased considerably as the war progressed although in Gloucester and Yorkshire the reverse was the case.

Given that regulations restricting child labour were relaxed before the end of the first month of the war, this is hardly surprising and was echoed in other sectors of society. The fact that child labour on the canals seems to have increased in some areas and decreased in others is a reflection of the different regional responses to the loss of boatmen to the armed forces. In Gloucester, it was stated by the school authorities that where the father had gone to the war, the rest of the family tended to remain at home and the children attended school.[187] This was probably the case in parts of Yorkshire also but in most areas traditionally dependent on family labour, the reverse was true with women and children taking the place of their absent men-folk. A deliberate effort on the part of the government to relieve labour shortages by recruiting female labour whenever unions would allow it[188] obviously increased this tendency. Thus, given that the heavy dependence on family labour, and in particular on child labour, lay at the root of most social evils on the canals, this was one respect in which government intervention as a result of the war actually acted as an obstacle to the improvement of social conditions for this sector of the population.

The Committee on Living-in on Canal Boats, 1920–1

WHEN in August 1919, the Transport Workers' Federation passed a resolution calling for the abolition of living-in on canal boats, both the Ministry of Health and the Board of Education appeared to welcome it and, on 12 November, a deputation from the Federation was received by a joint committee from both departments together with the Ministry of Transport. As a result, the Minister of Health, Christopher Addison, appointed a committee, under the chairmanship of Neville Chamberlain, to inquire into the practice of living-in on canal boats. The committee was not, however, appointed for another nine months and did not begin its work until November 1920. This delay may have reflected the political and personal difficulties being experienced at the time by Addison who was finding it increasingly difficult to find support in Cabinet for any radical social reforms. Lloyd George, who had lost much of his reformist zeal, tried to replace Addison in the spring of 1920 and actually succeeded in doing so twelve months later. It was against this background of hostility and uncertainty, therefore, that the enquiry took place.

During November and December 1920, the Committee heard evidence from twenty witnesses. Several canal carriers, missionaries, educationalists, inspectors, a midwife and a boatman were called (but no boat women). The unions, whose campaign had initiated the enquiry, declined to give evidence as a protest over the fact that no union representative was appointed to the Committee itself. Committee members also examined written evidence from witnesses and visited canal-boat wharves at Brentford and Paddington. Special surveys were commissioned at most of the main canal-boat depots throughout the country to find out the number of people living on canal boats, whether they had other homes ashore, how many school children were involved, whether they attended school and their degree of literacy.[189]

Witnesses tended to agree that children living on canal boats did suffer educationally as a result. As to the remedy, however, no such agreement could be reached. Many of the witnesses were against

36. Boat families at Braunston during a strike, which took place in 1923.
Ike Argent / Alan Faulkner Collection

37. Another view of striking boat people at Braunston during the dispute of 1923.
Ike Argent / Alan Faulkner Collection

prohibiting children from residing on board, the carriers on the grounds that it would lead to the abolition of the system of living-in and consequently the ruin of the industry, the missionaries on the grounds that it would break up family life. There was no clear evidence that the system of living-in was undesirable in other ways, for example on the grounds of health, cleanliness, morality or the safety of children and many of the witnesses felt that the presence of women on board was beneficial. They believed that the men were better fed, more sober and hard-working as a result.

Despite the fact that several of the witnesses had a vested interest in denying the practice of child labour, the evidence pointed clearly to its widespread existence. Even those who did deny it, admitted that children helped to a greater or lesser extent by steering and driving the horse. The assertion made by carriers[190] that boatmen would have to engage an extra hand if school-aged children were removed from the boats gives the lie to the claim that such children did not contribute materially to the operation of the trade.

The Committee reported early in 1921. Whilst

pointing to the difficulties they had experienced in obtaining reliable statistics and regretting the need to separate children from their parents, they nevertheless recommended that children between the ages of five and fourteen years should be prohibited from residing on board during school term time.

Two members of the Committee, H.J.R. Murray and Mrs Eleanor Barton, disagreed so strongly with the main report that they produced an addendum in which they condemned the whole practice of living-in in the strongest terms on grounds of health, and the general unsuitability of conditions on board for the rearing of young children.[191] They declared it to be their belief that young children were commonly forced to do work which was excessive and even cruel and they regretted the fact that insufficient weight had been given to the woman's point of view where living conditions on board were concerned.

This element of dissent greatly upset Chamberlain who felt that it reflected badly on his personal role as chairman and that anything less than a united front would weaken the effect of the report.[192] As a result, Murray and Barton were

65

obliged to greatly modify the tone of their addendum but they still made it clear that they felt the main report did not condemn the practice of living-in on canal boats strongly enough.

No further action on the report was taken however. By this time, Christopher Addison had been forced to resign from the Ministry of Health following difficulties over the cost of his housing policies and loss of personal power and support in the Cabinet. He was replaced by Alfred Mond, a wealthy businessman who had no inclination to innovate radical social policies of the type envisaged by the Living-in Committee's report. Furthermore, financial crisis developing over the winter of 1920–1 had removed social reform from the Parliamentary agenda for the foreseeable future.

Questions about the Committee's recommendations were raised in the House of Commons in 1922 and again in 1923 and 1926, but MP's were told that the time was not opportune for imposing new burdens on any branch of industry. Chamberlain himself became Minister of Health briefly in 1923 but even he found it politic not to resurrect the recommendations of his own committee. Housing shortages, political instability and financial crisis had ensured that no legislative solution would be immediately forthcoming.

The Paddington Basin refuse boats

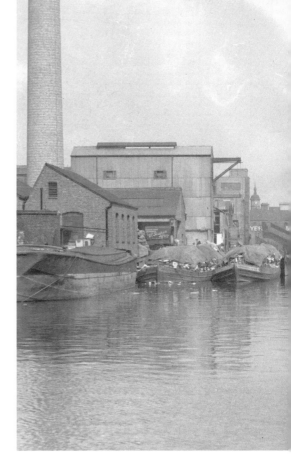

38. Paddington Basin in the 1930s.

Consequently, it fell to the civil servants to find an administrative solution. Between 1925 and 1930, the Ministry of Health toyed with the idea of making an Order under Section 2 of the Canal Boat Act 1877 to prohibit children from living on refuse boats in Paddington. The boats in question were mainly wide boats, some owned by private contractors and some by various West London councils. They carried house and street refuse from Paddington Basin to the refuse tips at West Drayton, a distance of some seventeen miles by canal. Investigations carried out in 1926 and 1930 showed that just over 100 children were resident on board.[193] As most of the boats were towed in trains by a steam tug, and as there were no locks on the journey, there appeared to be no necessity for family labour. Furthermore, as the journey was short, the men could have returned home each night thus removing the only other excuse for having families resident on board. Nevertheless, it was a long-standing custom for families to reside on these refuse boats. Although refuse boats on the Leeds and Liverpool Canal had cabins in which boatmen lived, in other cities – Birmingham, Manchester, Nottingham and Liverpool for example – refuse was transported by canal in open boats and thus no-one lived on board.

The campaign to remove children from Paddington boats was initiated by the Board of Education in a letter to the Ministry of Health in June 1925. They questioned the risk to health from the practice of children living on such boats and asked whether the Ministry could use its powers to prohibit it.[194]

heart.[196] On 23 March, he wrote to the Ministry of Health stating that the situation at Paddington was 'little short of a scandal' and enclosed a draft Order which would prohibit women and children from living on refuse boats. Llewellyn's action seems to have been prompted by fear of criticism from outside sources rather than a genuine concern for the welfare of the boat families. In the same report to the Ministry he wrote, 'we should have no proper defence if by any chance the question of their being allowed on the boats was raised'.

Ministry of Health officials found themselves in a difficult position. Their instinct was to avoid any radical new departure but they must also have been wary of ignoring their Chief Inspector's warning of possible criticism. A call for more information could not delay for long the need to act and in April the draft Order was referred to the Solicitors' Department for approval. Both Dawes and Ross, two Ministry of Health officials, seemed to be hoping for a legal objection. Ross himself suggested to the Solicitors' Department that the order might be *ultra vires* as 'it seems to go beyond anything done before' and his colleague Dawes added:

Unless we can say that the occupation of such boats is likely to cause the spread of infectious disease, I do not see how we can justify the making of a regulation under Section 2 [of the Canal Boats Act 1877].[197]

He also expressed doubt on the possibility of applying any new Order retrospectively to boats already registered under the Act.

Unfortunately for Dawes and Ross, the Solicitors' Department were not able to find the hoped-for legal obstacles. Gwyer, of the Solicitor's Department opined that the desired result could probably be achieved by restricting the occupants of refuse boats to nil and that any such Order could be applied to boats already registered. The only difficulty he foresaw was that of defining exactly the category of boat to which it was to apply. He nevertheless felt that the Ministry of Health had little to fear in going ahead, pointing out that:

… even if the legality of the regulation were subsequently challenged in the courts (which is not very probable) the Ministry would be unlikely to incur criticism of substance in view of the fact that the regulation has to lie in draft on the Table of both Houses for forty days before it can be made and if no

On being asked to investigate, Llewellyn declared himself against such a prohibition on the grounds that the contractors and boat people would object and the housing shortage in Paddington would not allow them to find accommodation ashore. He himself appeared to see nothing wrong with the practice at this time. The children were able to attend a special school when at Paddington and although they were surrounded by filth and completely lacked any washing facilities, their health did not appear to suffer. His advice was to 'let sleeping dogs lie' and to try to persuade the local authorities to provide washing facilities on the wharf.[195]

When consulted again in March 1926, he reported his position unchanged. Yet in the space of only a week he was to undergo a dramatic change of objection is taken to it during this prolonged period it can at any rate be assumed that it is made with the full approval of Parliament.[198]

Despite this reassurance, Ross wrote to Llewellyn on 14 May saying:

The legal position not being absolutely free from doubt we should require a strong case to justify the making of an order and I doubt whether we could proceed in the face of opposition.[199]

Bowing to the inclinations of his administrative superiors, Llewellyn quietly let the matter rest for the time being. During the summer of 1926, however, he received several letters from various local councils involved in the refuse-boat trade expressing their belief that the presence of children on the boats was both unnecessary and undesirable. Spurred on by this support, Llewellyn wrote again to the Ministry on 8 October stating that he had no hesitation in asking for an Order to have the children removed. However, while the Ministry prevaricated and suggested writing to the councils concerned to point out their duty to make proper

arrangements for refuse disposal, Llewellyn again allowed himself to be swayed from his intended path. In a letter to the Ministry dated 28 October, he reported on a meeting with Henry Boyer, the principal contractor involved, whom he described as a 'very nice and sensible fellow'. He rather credulously reported Boyer's claim that he continued to carry refuse by canal boat, even though he could transport it more cheaply by road, out of concern for the welfare of the boat people who would otherwise be thrown out of employment and recommended once again that the Order be dropped.

By March 1927, Llewellyn had once again grown concerned that the possibility of conditions at Paddington being exposed as a public scandal might bring down criticism upon the head of the department. He wrote:

As the condition of the children on the boats is so easily available to anyone who may care to enquire … I am concerned that the only way to get rid of the matter and any possible scandal arising out of it, is for the Ministry to make an Order removing the children, operative as

39. St Marylebone Borough Council's wide boat *Swallow* loaded with rubbish.
National Waterways Museum

68

soon as possible and consequently to remove the possibility of any 'press stunt' that may easily arise and for which we at present could have no satisfactory answer.[200]

The Ministry responded characteristically by requesting more information and in June, Llewellyn wrote again stating:

My main object is to prevent a newspaper 'stunt' concerning their presence on these filthy craft which would reflect no credit either on the Minister or the Inspector and might be the cause of 'panic' legislation resulting in the abolition of children from all boats which would be a pity.[201]

In July, an Order was once again put before the Solicitors' Department who this time decided that it could not be applied retrospectively. The question of enforcement was also raised in view of the fact that the only penalty for infringement would be a fine not exceeding twenty shillings. Once again, the idea of an Order was dropped and Llewellyn was left to try and press for washing facilities on the wharf.

In October 1927, he organised a meeting of interested parties. All agreed that the provision of washing facilities would be an excellent thing but when it came to the question of who was to provide for the cost of erection and upkeep, no progress could be made. In a passage which could easily have been written of cotton mill owners a hundred years earlier, Llewellyn reported:

The boat owners pointed out, quite correctly, that the health of these children could not be proved to suffer, that disease was scarce, that a certain and growing amount of education was received, that the children were learning a trade, that their parents were so well paid and lived in such circumstances that they were able to feed their children properly and probably to save money, as well as always being able to supervise them.

The Medical Officers of Health did not seem to care much what happened and declared themselves content whether the children remained on or were taken off the boats. It was suggested and declared an excellent suggestion on all sides that the canal wharf owner [who was not present] should build and maintain the wash houses.[202]

Predictably, Llewellyn had no more success persuading the wharf owners, the Grand Junction Canal Company, to provide washing facilities and the whole issue fell into abeyance. In September 1928, Llewellyn warned that conditions at Paddington were deteriorating, that the number of children on the boats appeared to be increasing and that the *Daily Mail* had discovered the existence of the refuse tips at the West Drayton end of the canal and could not long be kept away from Paddington. He was ignored by the Ministry of Health who seem to have resigned themselves to the idea that nothing more could be done by them to remedy the situation.

In February 1930, the Parliamentary Secretary to the Ministry of Health, Miss Susan Lawrence, visited Paddington Basin herself. Disgusted by what she saw, she urged Llewellyn to send written recommendations to the Department for remedying the situation. Llewellyn put forward six suggestions ranging from urging the boat owners or local authorities to remedy the problem to amending the Canal Boat Regulations in order to make it impossible for children to be accommodated on board. However, by this time a Private Member's Bill aimed at prohibiting children from living on any canal boat had begun its progress through Parliament and the Ministry saw no reason, for the present, to take action.

The Board of Education

DURING this period, the Board of Education gave consideration to various ways in which the educational difficulties of canal-boat children might have been addressed.

Up to 1926, there was no suggestion that the Board itself should take any direct action and it was able to confine itself to encouraging local education authorities to do what they could to improve the attendance of the children at school by sending attendance officers to the canal-side. Then in 1926, A. I. Dakin, the Inspector of Schools for Cheshire, made certain recommendations which concerned the Board directly and which show that the response of the Board to taking direct action was as cautious and conservative as that of the Ministry of Health.[203]

Dakin's first four recommendations concerned the organisation and teaching of children and did not involve the Board in any action, but his fifth and sixth points involved the making of regulations under the Education Act 1918 for the issuing of attendance books to the children. One official at the Board, D. Davidson, whilst agreeing that the power to issue such regulations existed, felt that it should not be done on the grounds that it had never been done before.[204]

The failure of the Board and the local authorities to co-operate and co-ordinate their efforts had a serious affect on later attempts to solve the problem of education for canal-boat children. In 1930, the London County Council made the seemingly sensible and harmless suggestion that education authorities concerned with the schooling of these children should confer and attempt to produce a common programme so that the children could move from one school to another with a greater deal of continuity of instruction.[205] The Council, not unreasonably, suggested that the initiative should come from the Board of Education but Davidson's response was to tell his superior, Pelham, that he did not see why the ball should not be returned to them [the London County Council].[206]

Earlier in the same minute, Davidson had revealed that what he really had in mind was to use the LCC's proposal to the Board's own advantage as a means of excusing it from taking any future action. He told his colleague:

The LCC idea of a conference … does contain the germ of a partial solution of the difficulty. If such a conference is called it would probably break up in failure, but it would have the advantage of showing that the Board had considered the possibility of administrative action to ameliorate the situation of these children and would definitely disprove the possibility of such an amelioration.

His colleague too felt that the scheme was impractical but felt that they ought to explore it further before turning it down. Accordingly, HMI Chambers was directed to make detailed investigations. He recommended setting up a National Council for the education of children and others connected with the canal-boat industry. It was to have the same status as a Local Education Authority and would co-ordinate schools and classes for these children throughout the country. Such an ambitious and innovative scheme was not likely to find favour with the deeply conservative officials of the Board and was quickly rejected.

The following year, however, the hoped-for conference between the LCC, the Middlesex County Council and the Board of Education did take place.[207] It was decided that the two schools at West Drayton and Paddington should, whilst remaining the financial and administrative responsibility of their respective education authorities, confer on curriculum content and agree a common programme. This limited scheme was the full extent of co-operation ever achieved by the Board amongst LEAS and there was never any attempt to extend it to other areas.

The Board now confined itself to the collecting of admittedly faulty statistics on forms which had remained unamended since the nineteenth century. It was found to be impossible to agree on an improved form[208] and it was felt to be not worth the effort anyway since nothing short of the impossible – i.e. the removal of all children from canal boats – would secure the adequate education of the canal-boat population. With that, the Board gave up, whether in despair or with relief is open to question, hoping and declaring itself to believe that with the decline of canal traffic the problem would solve itself.

The TGWU and the 'Boarding out' of canal-boat children

IN 1927, the Transport and General Workers' Union, under the leadership of Harry Gosling, renewed its interest in the education of canal-boat children and, in February 1928, Harry Gosling approached the Board of Education with a proposal to have the children boarded out during term time.[209] The Union's idea was that a boarding-out allowance should be made available to canal-boat parents to help them meet the cost of maintaining their children outside the family home and it offered to contribute to such an allowance from Union funds. The Board found that it had no powers to contribute financially itself to such a scheme but that there was provision under Section 23 of the Education Act 1918 for the Local Education Authorities to do so. In characteristic fashion, the Board welcomed any offer to solve the

40. Mrs Jane Nixon on *Matilda* or *Little Marvel*.
Leicester Evening Mail

problem of the education of canal-boat children which did not involve itself in direct responsibility for action and it circulated certain key authorities to ascertain their views. Not surprisingly, they replied that they were unable to contribute financially in the present circumstances. Not only was there the question of cost, but, as Wolverhampton pointed out, there was the possibility that relieving able-bodied parents in full employment of the responsibility of maintaining their own children would create a dangerous precedent.

When a deputation from the Union met the Parliamentary Secretary of the Board, the Duchess of Atholl, on 22 May 1928, it was stated that the use of public funds for such a purpose could not be justified until there was a real demand from the canal-boat people themselves for educational facilities. Gosling, claiming that his Union did indeed represent the wishes of the boat people, undertook to produce a few parents who would be willing to allow their children to take part in a boarding-out

scheme on an experimental basis. However, on 14 September, he was forced to admit, in a letter to the Board, that he had failed completely to get the support of the boat people for his scheme. Accordingly, he conceded the impossibility of solving the problem administratively and announced that his Union had resolved to seek a legislative solution through the introduction of a Private Member's Bill.

The Private Member's Bill of 1929

EARLY in 1929, Harry Gosling introduced his Bill which sought to ban all children below the age of fourteen years from travelling and residing on canal boats. This went further than the recommendation of the 1921 Committee on Living-in and the Ministry of Health felt:

… a manifest objection to doing anything which will

add to the demand for houses until more has been done to meet the present shortage.[210]

Believing that if children were removed from the boats the women would follow, and fearful of the consequences for the future of the industry, they were also concerned that:

… the Bill, if passed might … add a quota of unemployment, this just at a time when this particular business is said to be making headway after a long depression.

The Ministry therefore requested that the Bill be blocked on the grounds that it would need considerable modification and there would be no time to deal adequately with it in the current session.

The Bill failed to receive a second reading but, with the election of a Labour government in May 1929, Gosling determined to re-introduce it during the new session. Accordingly, he visited Charles Trevelyan, the new President of the Board of Edu-cation, in the hope of enlisting his support.[211] The President appears to have been sympathetic but said that the Bill was of the kind which might lead to it being obstructed and that therefore the government could not afford the time to take it up itself.

When the Bill came up for second reading on the 31 January 1930, Harry Nield MP,[212] alleging that the lack of educational facilities was imaginary, quoted a letter written by the Vicar of St Mary's Paddington who claimed that the boat children received all the education that was really necessary. The implication that such children did not really need much education at all was taken up by one of the Bill's supporters who also criticised Nield's claim that the children were healthier on boats than if they were living in Paddington:

If people are better off in barges than in Paddington slums, the remedy is not to keep them on barges but to improve the slums.

41. Laundering on board *Northolt* at Trent Lock in the early 1930s.
Ike Argent / Alan Faulkner Collection

Another supporter of the Bill felt that there was something very wrong with an industry which could only carry on by allowing a system which deprived its employees' children of education. He felt that in such a situation 'the State ought to step in and lay down the law that these things shall not be allowed'.

This raised the question of how far the State should go in regulating the lives of its citizens in the interest of the common good. Recognising this, the former President of the Board of Education, Lord Eustace Percy, felt that the Bill embodied a dangerous principle, 'an extension of the powers of compulsion which the country ought to refuse to accept'. He pointed out that legislation already existed to regulate the labours of children on canal boats but that the difficulty was enforcing it. The real issue which the Bill addressed was the need to put the population in a place where it could be properly inspected and this, he felt, was a very dangerous principle.

Percy felt that the Bill too closely resembled nineteenth-century ideas about protecting child workers in that it was a purely prohibitive measure. He thought that society had now moved on to the point that social legislation, instead of being compulsory and penal in its provisions, should be providing facilities to help parents achieve that which they naturally wanted for their children themselves. Accordingly, he called for boarding schools to be provided by local authorities, a measure which must have seemed rather extravagant and idealistic given the economic circumstances of the day.

The Bill received a second reading by a large majority but by the time it reached its third reading in May 1930, opposition to it had increased and its principal supporter, Harry Gosling, was dead. By now the committee stage had modified the Bill so that it applied only to school-aged children who were to be excluded during term-time but not at weekends, during school holidays or periods of certified sickness.[213]

Opposition came not only from those with vested business interests, such as the boat owners, who claimed that it would close the canals; voluntary agencies too found it unacceptable. The London City Mission and the Incorporated Seamen and Boatmen's Friend Society objected on the grounds that it would destroy family life. The London and National Society for Women's Service objected to the interference with the freedom of women involved in the clause excluding women from refuse boats.[214]

The boat people too voiced their objections. A group of them attended a meeting at the House of Commons on 5 May 1930 to protest about the Bill and a petition containing 1,006 signatures was presented to the House of Commons two days later.[215]

At the report stage and third reading of the Bill on 9 May, it was finally defeated. No further attempt to reform social conditions on canal boats by legislative means was ever made. The provisions of the nineteenth-century Canal Boats Acts were re-enacted in the Public Health Act of 1936 and the welfare of the boating population continued to be governed by legislation which had already proved to be inadequate before the end of the previous century.

The 1930s

WITH the failure of Gosling's Bill, canal-boat social policy entered a decade of quiescence and even complacency. By 1936, some disquiet about the educational difficulties began to reach the Board of Education once again but it was brushed aside. Whilst privately noting that the arrangements for educating canal-boat children were still far from adequate, the Board was reluctant to admit as much to outside agencies.[216] When the National Union of Conservative and Unionist Associations complained in April 1936 that the education regulations concerning canal-boat children were not being enforced, the Board replied that its annual returns from local authorities did not bear out such a claim. In January 1937, *The Star* publicly accused the Board of complacency. This, and similar complaints from the Association of Superintendents of School Attendance Departments, failed to move the officials of the Board. They contented themselves with the notion that, as the number of children on boats seemed to be decreasing, the problem could be said to be solving itself and that furthermore, previous experience of attempts at legislation was not encouraging.

At the Ministry of Health a similar atmosphere prevailed. Owen Llewellyn retired in 1931 and was not replaced. When the Board of Education requested the Ministry's help in revising their form for collecting information on canal-boat children, the Ministry declined to assist, admitting that there was now no-one in the department who knew much about canals.[217]

The success of the newly formed Grand Union Canal Carrying Company and its plans to expand further and build a new fleet of narrow boats did prompt some activity at the Ministry of Health. In December 1934, an office committee was set up to consider revising the regulations governing standards of accommodation on boats registered as dwellings.[218] However, the committee members confined themselves to structural features of the boats, particularly the ventilation of the cabins in view of the advent of motor traction. They were warned by A.M. Legge of the Ministry to 'be aware of the previous history on other points' and to 'steer clear of points to do with the educational aspect of children'.

The committee spent six months collecting facts and produced an interim report in June 1935. It then adjourned for more than two years and resumed in November 1937. A new set of statutory regulations was drafted in 1938. The main changes were new regulations concerning the ventilation of motor boats and an increase in the air space required in the cabin to 100 cubic feet per person. The regulations were never implemented. Legge later blamed this on the outbreak of the Second World War.[219]

The Second World War

A T THE outbreak of war, the Ministry of Transport set up the Canals (Defence) Advisory Committee. This was concerned mainly with labour shortages and the financial difficulties of the carriers. Financial assistance given to carriers and canal companies prevented many going out of business and helped to prevent the living standards of boat families from falling too far behind those of other workers. Extra shops, canteens and iron rations helped to relieve some of the war-time hardships of canal life.[220]

The war-time training scheme for women has already been mentioned. Many of those who came to work on the canals at that time were educated middle-class women who had probably had little previous contact with working-class families. They were shocked by the conditions of life among the traditional boat population and communicated their disquiet to Sir Osborne Mance, the war-time Director of Canals. On 23 August 1943, Mance contacted Howell James at the Ministry of Health to express his concern that boat people were not receiving the medical treatment and welfare amenities to which they were entitled.[221]

After more than a decade of quiescence in the area of canal-boat social policy, the Ministry of Health officials were irritated at the prospect of this old hornets' nest being reopened and they adopted a highly defensive stance at the suggestion of criticism from another Ministry. One disgruntled official was moved to write 'The Ministry of War Transport seem to think we have never heard of canal boats!'[222]

A similar note of irritation and resentment is evident in the report of a meeting which took place between the two Ministries on 14 September 1943. The Health Ministry officials reported that Mance

… was not prepared to accept the experience of the past seventy years that the social and economic conditions of canal boats in fact worked and were satisfactory to the population concerned,

and accused him of 'generalising from extremely slight evidence' which he had obtained from the voluntary trainees who 'told him things'.

Ministry of War Transport papers record the extreme reluctance with which the Ministry of Health had agreed to this meeting:

He [Legge] is the only person at the Ministry of Health with information about canal boat legislation but his knowledge did not extend to medical arrangements. He knew of no-one in the Ministry who would be in a position to talk on this subject in relation to canal personnel. No regulations have been made by the Ministry of Health under the Public Health Act and the regulations in force prior to that Act were still applicable. The only Ministry of Health inspector of canal boats had retired some time ago and his place had not been filled.

Mr Legge obviously wished to avoid a meeting. He suggested that we were stirring up a matter which the

Ministry of Health had found desirable to leave acquiescent having regard to the peculiarities of the individuals concerned. I pressed him very strongly and ultimately he agreed to endeavour to find others in his Ministry who would discuss the questions likely to be raised.[223]

At the prompting of the Ministry of War Transport, the Ministry of Health undertook to investigate the provision of medical facilities in general and infant and maternity welfare provision in particular. After extensive investigations, including visits to various narrow-boat depots on the Grand Union Canal, an official from the Ministry of Health, N.B. Battenbury, concluded that public health activities among canal-boat people had been allowed to lapse and, in fact, had never been very satisfactory.[224] Following this, some effort was made, particularly at the London end of the Grand Union Canal, to see that expectant mothers received ante-natal and post-natal care.

The difficulties experienced recruiting men and women to relieve the labour shortages on the canals during the war also focused attention on the conditions of employment in the canal carrying industry. The Ministry of Labour held the view that the wages and conditions of employment for boat crews were so unsatisfactory that the employment should not be protected by the Essential Work Order until they were set right.[225] The system of families living-in on boats and the absence of any specific wage apportionment to the crew were held to be particular evils. Pressure to remedy the situation led, in 1943, to the setting up of a Joint Industrial Council for the Inland Waterways Industry. Although it was found impossible to abolish the family labour system or even to apportion a specific wage to crews of narrow boats except on the canals between Birmingham and the Severn, significant reforms were made in other areas. For the first time, national agreements were made on wage rates for long distance and short distance boatmen and agreements were made on minimum weekly wages and demurrage payments.[226]

After the Second World War, responsibility for administering the provisions of the Public Health Act as they related to canal-boat dwellings passed to the Ministry of Housing and Local Government. The department might have been content to forget

42. Mary Nixon at the tiller of *Daphne* on the Ashby Canal in March 1956. *Leicester Evening Mail*

the existence of such responsibilities, but in 1957 the local public health authority for Northamptonshire wrote apologising for the fact that they had not sent in their annual report on canal boats as required under the Act. The Ministry then discovered to its embarrassment that no-one had ever looked at such reports for years.[227]

The issue of state intervention on behalf of canal-boat people was kept alive during the 1950s by the activities of the canal-boat inspector and town clerk of Runcorn with the assistance of their local MP Dennis Vosper.[228] In 1950 they urged that a new set of regulations be drawn up laying down improved standards of sanitation etc. on board. After long delays a new set of regulations was drawn up in November 1955 and circulated for comment. However, by the time this process was complete, in September 1957, it was decided that there was no longer any point in going ahead due to the dwindling number of people still resident on canal boats.

Epilogue

So why did so much activity achieve so little? First of all, one has to keep in mind the enormity of the problem and to ask what *could* have been done anyway? The choice seems to have been between taking a bold approach which would sweep away the problem altogether, i.e. abolish the family boat system completely, or adopt a more cautious approach and try to bring about small improvements on an *ad hoc* basis by administrative means and by patching up the existing legislation.

No attempt at the first approach was made by central government departments. The one attempt by outside agencies to introduce a Bill failed and this approach was completely abandoned by the 1930s. Such a drastic measure was never likely to succeed in the circumstances of the inter-war period. The Ministry of Health, on whose shoulders it would have fallen to administer new legislation, was in no state to initiate innovative and controversial measures, at least, not after the departure of Christopher Addison with his housing policy in tatters. The frequent changes of Minister throughout the 1920s meant that the department lacked strong leadership during a period which was, in any case, characterised by political instability and financial crisis. Furthermore, the department was staffed by officials who were conservative, fearful of treading new ground and who preferred to do nothing rather than embark on a course of action which ran the smallest risk of failure or of incurring criticism of the department.

The efforts of reformers received little support from the boat people themselves. Many made it quite clear that they did not want to leave their boats, or have their children boarded out. Reforms involving such measures, which touched on important fundamental questions about society, were seen as less than desirable by other people too. Not only did they run against traditional attitudes which emphasised the responsibility of the individual for himself and his dependents, the sanctity of the family and the concern not to interfere with com-petitive industry, but they raised the question of the desirability of the extension of state power.

Short of abolishing the use of family labour on boats, there seem to have been a number of measures which could have been taken to alleviate the deprivations of canal-boat people. The main difficulty here was that local authorities played a crucial role in the provision of social services and boat people, moving around the country as they did, could not be deemed to be the responsibility of any particular authority.

The records of the Board of Education and the Ministry of Health leave one feeling that more could have been done to help boat people. In particular, the Board of Education could have co-operated more closely with its local education authorities and one is left in no doubt that certain officials at the Ministry of Health found canal-boat administration an irritating nuisance which, if ignored, might solve itself. It is hard to see any real justification for the inordinate length of time taken to achieve any action, for example the drafting of new canal-boat regulations. One cannot help feeling that this was merely a delaying tactic to enable a reluctant department to avoid facing its responsibilities.

Yet one has also to bear in mind the sheer enormity of tasks facing social policy makers and implementers at the time. Priorities had to be drawn up and if one accepts one modern historian's view that these priorities were based on the promotion of economic efficiency and social stability rather than altruism, then it is not surprising that a small group of conservative, largely unorganised people in a declining industry were of little concern to politicians and administrators.

Of course, by the post-war period their numbers were dwindling. Nevertheless, the fact that the use of family labour on boats continued until 1970 meant that, during a period of universal welfare provision, a whole generation – perhaps as many as 2,000 people – were denied even a basic education or the bare minimum of modern living standards.

References

Chapter One

1. Gerard Turnball, 'Canals, coal and regional growth during the industrial revolution,' *Economic History Review,* 2nd ser. XL,4 (1987), p.543, note 21.
   – R.B. Dunwoody, 'Inland Water Transport,' a paper read before the Economic Section of the British Association at Birmingham on 12.9.1913, p.10.
2. Ibid.
3. Turnbull, 'Canals, coal and regional growth,' p.543.
4. For further details *see* Harold Crabtree, edited by Mike Clarke, *Railway on the Water, 'Tom Puddings' and the Yorkshire Coal Industry,* (1994).
5. PRO RAIL 855/156 p.58, Oxford Canal Company, list of men employed on the Oxford Canal, September 1853.
6. Minutes of Evidence of The Select Committee to enquire into the expediency of restraining the practice of carrying goods and merchandise on Canals and Navigable rivers and Railways on Sundays, *House of Lords Journal,* 4th and 5th Victoria, 1841, Vol. 73, (S.C. on Sunday Trading), appendix 2, p.208.
7. Royal Commission on Canals and Inland Navigations in the United Kingdom PP (1906–9), vol 1, part 2, [Cd.3183–4], XXXII, qq.4431–2.
8. S.C. on Sunday Trading, 1841, qq.532–3.
9. Report and Evidence of the Select Committee on Canals, PP 1883, (252), XIII, q.2619.
10. S.C. on Sunday Trading, 1841, q.1261.
11. G. Turnball, 'Pickfords and the canal carrying trade, 1780–1850,' in *Transport History,* vol. 6, 1973, p.12.
12. S.C. on Railway and Canal Bill, 1852–3, q.1596.
13. Ibid, q.1148.
14. Report and Evidence of the Select Committee on the Canal Boats Act (1877) Amendment Bill, PP 1884 (263), VIII, (S.C. on Canal Boats Bill), q.1288.
    – Report and Evidence of the Select Committee on Canals, PP 1883, (252) XIII, qq.2666–7.
15. For a full account of the rise and decline of canal carrying *see* Edward Paget-Tomlinson, *The illustrated history of canal and river navigations* (1993 edn) and L.J. Boughey, *Charles Hadfield's British canals* (1994).
16. Factory and Workshops Act Commission, PP 1876 [C1443], XXIX, Vol 1, Appendix C, p.124.
17. Harry Hanson, *The Canal Boatmen 1760–1914,* (1975; 1984 edition), pp.53–5.
18. John Hassell, *A Tour of the Grand Junction Canal in 1819* (1819; 1968 reprint), p.45.
19. Report and Evidence of the Select Committee on the Observance of the Sabbath Day PP 1831–2 (697), VIII, q.1829.
20. S.C. on Sunday Trading, 1841, qq.619, 1220.
21. Census of Great Britain 1851, Vol 11 Part 1, Population tables: Ages, civil condition, Occupations and Birthplaces, 1854, table xxv.
22. The counties selected were: Bedfordshire, Buckinghamshire, Cheshire, Derbyshire, Hereford, Hertfordshire, Lancashire, Leicestershire, Middlesex (but not London), Northamptonshire, Nottinghamshire, Oxfordshire, Shropshire, Staffordshire, Warwickshire, Worcestershire and West Yorkshire. Admittedly, this selection will have excluded some canal boatmen and included quite a few river boatmen, especially on the Thames and the Mersey.
23. S.C. on Canal Boats Act (1877) Amendment Bill, 1884, Appendix 1.
24. Evidence that boatmen had homes ashore can be found in the following documents:
    – S.C. on Sunday Trading, 1841, qq.334–5, 364, 922–30.
    – Factory and Workshops Act Commission, 1876, Vol 1, Appendix C.
    – S.C. on Canal Boats Act (1877) Amendment Bill, 1884, qq.343–5, 1140, 1189–91,
    – PRO ED 11/89, Precis of reports from local school attendance officers, 1908.
    – PRO ED 11/89 Private papers of H.J.R. Murray, Board of Education, 1920–1.
    – Inter-departmental Committee on Living in on Canal Boats, 1921–1, q.983, 1222, 2288, 2235 (and others).
    – *Child's Guardian,* (NSPCC newspaper), January 1930.
    – PRO HLG 52/1094 Report of N.B. Battenbury, Ministry of Health, 3.1.1944.

Chapter Two

25. Royal Commission on Labour (group B), Transport and Agriculture, vol III, PP 1893–4 [C.6894-VIII], XXXIII, qq.12109–11, 15153–7, 15389–92, 15466–68, 15587–95, 15697–99.
26. Ibid. 15469–73.
27. S.C. on Sunday Trading, 1841, q.556–7.
28. Ibid, q.516.
29. PRO MT 52/2 Report on the proceedings of the Canal Control Committee, undated, *c.* July 1919.
30. PRO LAB 83/2494, Midland Canal Boatmen's Wages Board, terms of settlement with boatmen, 28.5.1920.
31. PRO LAB 83/2494 Industrial Court Minutes, 27.4.1921.
32. PRO LAB 83/2483 Blackburn & District Coal Owners Association, Boat-owners minutes, 11.8.1947.
33. PRO RAIL 623/28 Shropshire Union Canal & Railway Company, Executive Committee Minutes, minute no.25454, 28.7.1920.
34. PRO LAB 83/2479 North East Regional Joint Council for the Canal Industry, meeting held 27.7.1945.
35. *Waterways,* house magazine of the British Transport Waterways, August 1959.
36. Ibid. May 1960.
37. David Blagrove, *Bread Upon the Waters,* (1984) p.39.
38. Ibid. p.23.
39. Author of *Hold On a Minute,* interviewed by W. Freer, 11.8.1988.
40. H. Hanson, *Canal People,* (1978), p.67.
41. T. W. Cubbon, *Only a little cockboat,* (1928), quoted in H. Hanson, *Canal People,* p.73.
42. Harry Fletcher, *A Life on the Humber: Keeling to Shipbuilding,* (1975), p.60.
43. H. Hanson, *The Canal Boatmen, 1760–1914,* p.42.
44. *Standard,* 8.9.1877.
45. PRO RG 10/3089, 3100, vessels at Worcester Wharf and Crescent Wharf.
46. PRO RG 9/3, p.189–258.
47. Report and Evidence taken before the Committee appointed by the Minister of Health to Inquire into the Practice of Living-in on Canal Boats in England and Wales and to Report Whether any Alteration in the Practice is Desirable, 1920–1. For further information about this committee *see* chapter 6.
48. PRO ED 11/88. *See also* chapter 4.
49. R. C. on Labour, 1892, qq.12119–25.
50. Ibid. qq.15270–89.
51. PRO MT 52/102 Ministry of War Transport, Canal Labour, General File, 9.5.1942.
52. PRO MT 52/90 Central Canal Committee, 32nd meeting, 15.2.1945.
53. PRO MT 52/102 Ministry of War Transport, Canal Labour, General File, 6.11.1942.
54. PRO MT 52/90 Central Canal Committee, 32nd meeting 15.2.1945.
55. S.C. on Sunday Trading, 1841, qq.626–9.
56. Ibid, qq.1053–163.
57. Ibid, qq.216–20.
58. Factory and Workshop Commission, PP, 1876, XXX, qq.1127–82.
59. Board of Trade, Report of an Enquiry into the Earnings and Hours of Work People in the United Kingdom in 1906, PP, 1912–13, CVIII.
60. PRO MT 21/1, Minutes of the Canal Control Committee, 1.6.1917 refers to and quotes from correspondence placed before the committee regarding widespread discontent in the industry.
    – PRO LAB 34/29–38, Strikes and lockouts, 1911–20.
61. PRO MT 52/5, Transcript of a conference between the Ministry of Transport and representatives of the Canal Association, 22.7.1920.
62. PRO MT 52/14, R.B. Dunwoody, *Vernon Harcourt Lecture,* 1920, p.40.
63. PRO LAB 83/2494, Industrial Court Minutes, 27.4.1921.
64. PRO LAB 83/2496, Industrial Court Minutes, 20.11.1923.
65. PRO LAB 83/2492, Award in the matter of arbitration between the Trent Navigation Company Ltd and the Transport and General Workers Union, 20.7.1936.
66. PRO HLG 52/140 MOH Paddington to Chief Inspector Llewellyn, 25.10.1926.

Chapter Three

67. PRO HLG 52/1094 Health Visitor's report for Waterloo Wharf, Uxbridge, 17.1.1946.
68. Quoted in *Our Canal Population,* George Smith, 1875.
69. PRO MT 52/102 Letter to Sir Osborne

Mance, Director of Canals, from Mrs Butson, war-time trainee, 22.1.1942.

70. John Liddle, Medical Officer of Whitechapel, Sanitary Report, (Supplement) for Whitechapel, 1842.

71. John Burnett, *A Social History of Housing, 1815–1970,* (1978) p.67.

72. Thomas Beames, *The Rookeries of London,* (1852) and Report on the Employment of Women and Children in Agriculture, 1843, referred to in Burnett, *A Social History of Housing,* p.64 and p.23.

73. First Report of the Royal Commission of Enquiry into the Housing of the Working Classes with Evidence, PP 1884–5 [C.4402–1], XXXI, p.10.

74. John Hollingshead, 'On the Canal,' published in *Household Words,* 1858, reprinted in 1973 by the Waterways Museum, Stoke Bruerne, p.47. *Birmingham Daily Mail,* 12.3.1876.

75. For further information about these Acts *see* chapter 5.

76. PRO HLG 52/141 Report of R.F. Evans, Ministry of Health, on new canal boats being built for the Grand Union Canal Carrying Company, 17.1.1935.

77. PRO HLG 52/141 Report of Dr W.S. Craig to Ministry of Health 3.1.1937.

78. PRO RAIL 830/23 Grand Junction Canal Company, Board Minutes, 9.10.1889, p.332.

79. Committee on living-in, 1920–1, q.1046 and 1557.

80. PRO HLG 52/1094 Report of N.B. Battenbury to the Ministry of Health, 3.1.1944.

81. PRO ED 11/90 Report of Dr Wilson to the Ministry of Health, 30.8.1927.

82. PRO HLG 52/1094 Report to the Ministry of Health 3.1.1944.

83. *Waterways,* July 1960.

84. Political and Economic Planning Survey on Household Appliances 1945, quoted in M.J. Daunton, *House and Home in the Victorian City,* (1983) pp.242–4.

85. Mrs Tim Wilkinson, interviewed by W. Freer, 11.8.1988.

86. Hollingshead, *On the Canal,* p.44.

87. *Birmingham Daily Mail,* 12.3.1875.

88. PRO MT 52/61 Central Canal Committee minutes, 20.11.1941.

89. S.C. on Sunday Trading, 1841, qq.89, 487, 488, 489, 806, 869.

90. *The Waterman,* magazine of the Incorporated Seamen and Boatmen's Friend Society, March 1910.

91. Sixth Annual Report of the Canal Boatmen's Mission and Day School, 1902, (Found on PRO ED 11/40).

92. *The Waterman,* December 1910 and other issues.

93. 'Floating School', *Manchester Guardian,* 30.9.1930.

94. PRO MT 52/109 Frank Pick report to Minister of War Transport, 1941, para 86.

95. PRO RAIL 623/19 Shropshire Union Canal & Railway Company, Executive Committee Minutes, minute 11958, 24.10.1877.

96. Ibid, minute 25691, 14.12.1921.

97. PRO RAIL 52/109 Frank Pick report to the Ministry of War Transport, 1941, para 86.

98. PRO RAIL 1005/315 Minutes of the Committee of Management of the Liskeard & Looe Union Canal Company, 2.9.1825.

99. PRO HLG 52/1094 Report of N.B. Battenbury to the Ministry of Health, 31.1.1944.

100. PRO HLG 52/1094 Report of the Elementary Education and General Purposes Sub-committee, London County Council, July 1930.

101. PRO HLG 52/1094 Report of N.B. Battenbury to the Ministry of Health, 31.1.1944.

102. Interview of Dr Smith's daughter by W. Freer, August 1988.

103. Sixth Annual Report of the Canal Boatmen's Mission and Day School, 1902.

104. Committee on Living-in, 1920–1.

105. PRO HLG 52/1094 Dr Lillian Wilson, October 1930.

106. PRO HLG 52/1094.

107. Ibid.

108. PRO HLG 32/94, first report of the Chief Canal Boat Inspector, Sept/Dec 1884.

109. PRO MH 32/94 Letter from John Robertson, MOH Birmingham, to the Committee on Living-in, 1921.

110. E.C. Buchanan Tudor, Engineer & Surveyor to the Local Government Board, Goole, to the District Meeting of the Association of Municipal and Sanitary Engineers & Surveyors, Tynemouth, 27.9.1882. (Hadfield papers, 10/8, LSE)

111. Committee on Living-in, 1921, q.354 and appendix L para 7.

112. PRO HLG 52/1094 Miss P.M. Bucknall, Ministry of Health on a visit to the Grand Union Canal Carrying Company yard, North Hyde, 26.1.1944.

113. Ibid. Health Visitor, Uxbridge, 17.1.1946.

114. Ibid, Report of N.B. Battenbury to the Ministry of Health, 31.1.1944.

115. Ibid.

116. Ibid, Report of the General Purposes Sub-committee, London County Council Education Committee, July 1930.

117. Ibid, Report of Dr Wilson on her visit to the canal boat class, Paddington, 30.8.1927.

118. For further details *see* chapter 6.

Chapter Four

119. Evidence of the S.C. on Canal Boats Act (1877) Amendment Bill, 1884, q.206.

120. PRO ED 11/88–9, returns to the Board of Education from LEAs.

121. Evidence of the S.C. on Sunday Trading, 1841, qq.616–7.

122. Ibid. q.806.

123. Ibid. q.869.

124. *The Waterman,* magazine of the Incorporated Seamen and Boatmen's Friend Society, March 1910.

125. W.E. Marsden, *Unequal Educational Provision in England and Wales, the Nineteenth-century roots,* London, 1987, p.28.

126. Reports from the Factory Inspectors on the Educational Provisions of the Factory Acts, PP 1839, XLII, p.353.

127. For more details of the Canal Boats Acts *see* Chapter 5.

128. PRO RAIL 623/22–8, Shropshire Union Canal & Railway Company, Executive Committee Minutes, 1900–22. For example, 14.11.1900 minute 21662, 14.10.1903 minute 22099, 18.6.1919 minute 23035, 16.6.1920 report of officers' conference.

129. PRO RAIL 860/86 Grand Union Canal Company Minutes, minute 13607, 27.11.1929.

130. PRO ED 11/88. Minute dated 16.6.1919.

131. For more information *see* chapter 6.

132. PRO ED 11/237, National Association of Inland Waterways Carriers' memorandum, 9.2.1945.

133. PRO ED 11/89. *The Schoolmaster (Women's Supplement),* 20.7.1918.

134. Committee on Living-in, 1921, q.220.

135. PRO ED 11/90 Report of A.I. Dakin to the Board of Education on canal-boat children in Cheshire, August/September 1926.

136. Ibid.

137. PRO ED 11/89. Written evidence submitted to the Committee on Living-in, 1920.

138. PRO HLG 52/1094.

139. Committee on Living-in, 1920–21, q.2269.

140. PRO ED 11/92, Report of HMI Ball, 8.5.1930.

141. PRO ED11/92. HMI Chambers, 22.10.1930.

142. Committee on Living-in, 1921, q.236.

143. PRO ED 11/89, written evidence to the Committee on Living in, 1920–1, Dr Donald Fraser, clerk to the Runcorn Education Authority Sub-committee.

144. *The Waterman,* March 1910, March 1948.

145. PRO ED 11/88, Report of C.H. Sittington to the Board of Education, 4.2.1920.

146. Ibid.

147. PRO ED 11/91, Report of M. Baker, teacher in charge of Brentford Canal Boat Class, 12.1.1928.

148. PRO ED 11/92.

149. PRO ED 11/1094, Dr L. Wilson, 10–16.10.1930.

150. PRO HLG 52/1094, report of Micklewright.

151. Ibid. report of N.B. Battenbury, 31.1.1944.

152. Ibid. Battenbury minute 16.2.1945 and report of MOH Chiswick, 7.5.1946.

153. PRO ED 11/92, report of HMI Chambers, 22.10.1930.

154. PRO HLG 52/135, report dated 13.2.1930.

155. PRO HLG 52/1094, report of N.B. Battenbury, 31.1.1944.

156. PRO ED 11/92, letter from Middlesex Education Committee to the Board of Education, 23.4.1931.

157. *Waterways,* May 1959.

Chapter Five

158. For example, *see* Jennifer Hart, 'Nineteenth-century Social Reform: a Tory Interpretation of History,' *Past and Present,* No.31, (1965).

159. S.C. on Sunday Trading, 1841, qq.84, 109–10, 579, and 872.
160. Edwin Hodder, *George Smith of Coalville, The Story of an Enthusiast,* (1896).
161. George Smith, *Our Canal Population,* (1875, reprinted 1975, pp.11–15)
162. Factory and Workshop Commission, 1875, William Leese and William Ollier, qq.10868–916.
163. Ibid. q.12874.
164. George Smith, article published in the *Argonaut,* September 1875, reproduced in *Our Canal Population,* pp.93–112. Smith's recommendations appear on p.105.
165. Evidence of the S.C. on the Canal Boat Act (1877) Amendment Bill, 1884, Appendix 5, paper handed in by George Smith on the operation of the 1877 Act.
166. Ibid. qq.677 and 698–706 (child labour and education), 708–12 (indecent occupation of boats), 740–53 (spread of disease), 754–7 (indecency), 856 (illegitimate children).
167. Ibid. qq.930–35.
168. PRO MH 32/94, Local Government Board Inspectors' Correspondence.
169. 39th Report of the Local Government Board, 1909 (1910) part II [Cd.5275], XXXVIII, appendix, report of the Chief Canal Boat Inspector, p.76.
– 31st Report of the Local Government Board, 1901 (1902) [Cd.1231], XXV, p.166.
170. 35th Annual Report of the Local Government Board, 1905 (1906) [Cd.3105], XXXV.
171. PRO ED 11/40, Northwich Rural District Council to the Board of Education, 14.2.1905.
172. 36th Annual Report of the Local Government Board, 1906 (1907) [Cd.3665], XXVI, appendix, report of the Chief Canal Boat Inspector, p.59.
173. Richard Parr, *Canal Boat Children,* NSPCC, (1910), p.30.
174. PRO ED 11/1 replies to circular 283 on the education of canal boat children, replies from Birmingham, 26.5.1883, 1.6.1887, and 6.6.1893.
175. Ibid.
176. Ibid.
177. PRO ED 11/88, J. Doig McGrindle, Assistant Medical Officer of Health, Birmingham. Report of the conditions of life under which canal-boat children, especially those of school age (5–14 years) are reared, 27.2.1906.
178. PRO ED 11/88, James H. Broscom, District Inspector of Schools, City of Birmingham Education Committee, Report on the educational condition of children found in connection with canal boats lying at various wharves within the city of Birmingham, 1904–5.

179. Annual Report of the Board of Education, 1902–3 (1903) [Cd.1763], XX 349, p.46.
180. Richard Parr, *Canal Boat Children.*

Chapter Six

181. PRO MT 52/1, Canal Control Committee, 15.6.1917.
182. Ibid.
183. Ibid.
184. Ibid. Report of a meeting which took place at the Ministry of Shipping, 7.6.1917.
185. PRO MT 52/3 Weekly reports to the Board of Trade by the Canal Control Committee, 13.8.1919. PRO MT 52/2, Minutes of the Canal Control Committee, 6.9.1918 and 12.9.1919.
186. PRO MT 52/1 Minutes of Canal Control Committee, 22.2.1918.
187. PRO ED 11/88 notes on the canal-boat registers of Archdeacon School, Gloucester, submitted to the Board of Education in 1919.
188. PRO MT 52/1, *see* for example minutes 1.6.1917.
189. PRO ED 11/89 the private papers of H.J.R. Murray, HMI, Board of Education and a member of the Committee on Living-in, 1921.
190. Committee on Living-in, 1920–1, qq.341–9.
191. PRO ED 11/89 private papers of H.J.R. Murray.
192. Ibid. Letter from Neville Chamberlain to Murray, 15.3.1921.
193. PRO HLG 52/135 letter from G.E. Oates, MOH Paddington to W.A. Ross, Ministry of Health, 14.3.1930.
194. PRO HLG 52/140 letter from Cleary, Board of Education to W.A. Ross, Ministry of Health, 12.6.1925.
195. Ibid. Report by Chief Canal Boat Inspector, 17.7.1925.
196. Ibid. Minute of 15.3.1926.
197. Ibid. Ministry of Health departmental minute, 30.3.1926.
198. Ibid. Minutes of 4.5.1926 and 7.5.1926 by Gwyer of the Solicitors' Department.
199. Ibid.
200. Ibid. Llewellyn to Ross, 7.3.1927.
201. Ibid. Llewellyn to Ross 14.6.1927.
202. PRO ED 11/90, Report by Llewellyn, 31.10.1927.
203. Ibid. Report of A.I. Dakin, August/September 1926.
204. Ibid. Departmental minute, Davidson to Pelham, 3.11.1930.
205. PRO ED 11/92 Letter from London County Council to E.H. Pelham, Board of Education, 31.7.1930.
206. Ibid. Departmental minute from Davidson to Pelham, 3.11.1930.

207. Ibid. Report of Canal Boat Conference, 9.7.1931.
208. Ibid. *See* for example Cambell's minute to Ainsworth, 18.6.1931, para 4a.
209. PRO ED 11/91, report on a meeting between Gosling and Board of Education, 25.2.1928.
210. PRO HLG 52/135 Ministry of Health memorandum on the Second Reading of the Bill.
211. PRO ED 11/91 Board of Education interview memorandum, 1.8.1929.
212. Parliamentary Debates, Vol. 234, No. 72, 1403–4.
213. PRO ED 24/1122 Canal Boats Bill Standing Committee B, Amendments.
214. Ibid. Statement by the Incorporated Seamen & Boatmen's Friend Society, 24.2.1930 and letter from the London & National Society for Women's Service to Morgan Jones MP, 6.5.1930.
215. Ibid. Circular to MPs giving notice of the meeting 2.5.1930.
– Memo from A.M. Currie, Private Secretary to HMI Ball, 6.5.1930. *Manchester Guardian,* 30.9.1930.
216. PRO ED 11/237 Board of Education departmental minute, Lasky to Cleary, 5.11.1936.
217. Ibid. Board of Education departmental minute, Davidson to Ainsworth, 12.8.1931.
218. PRO HLG 52/141 Ministry of Health, Regulations Reports, General Inspectors' Office Committee.
219. PRO HLG 52/1636 Ministry of Health, departmental minute, A.M. Legge, 11.6.1941.
220. PRO MT 52/59 Central Canal Committee.
221. PRO HLG 52/1094 Letter from Sir Osborne Mance, Ministry of War Transport to the Ministry of Health, 23.8.1943.
222. Ibid. Ministry of Health, departmental minute, 11.9.1943.
223. PRO MT 52/134 Ministry of War Transport, departmental minute by W.J. Shea between 23.8.1943 and 14.9.1943.
224. PRO HLG 52/1094 Ministry of Health report by N.B. Battenbury.
225. PRO MT 52/109 Frank Pick report to the Ministry of War Transport, 14.5.1921.
– PRO MT 52/55 Ministry of War Transport, Canals General Policy, minute 19.7.1940.
226. For example PRO LAB 83/2493 and LAB 83/2498.
227. PRO HLG 52/1412 Ministry of Housing and Local Government departmental minute, Chipperfield to Devey, 16.9.1957.
228. Ibid. Various pieces of correspondence on this file.

Index